CHARLOTTE AND EMILY BRONTË

Macmillan Literary Lives
General Editor: Richard Dutton, Senior Lecturer in English,
University of Lancaster

This series offers stimulating accounts of the literary careers of the most widely read British and Irish authors. Volumes follow the outline of writers' working lives, not in the spirit of traditional biography, but aiming to trace the professional, publishing and social contexts which shaped their writing. The role and status of 'the author' as the creator of literary texts is a vexed issue in current critical theory, where a variety of social, linguistic and psychological approaches have challenged the old concentration on writers as specially-gifted individuals. Yet reports of 'the death of the author' in literary studies are (as Mark Twain said of a premature obituary) an exaggeration. This series aims to demonstrate how an understanding of writers' careers can promote, for students and general readers alike, a more informed historical reading of their works.

Series Standing Order

If you would like to receive future titles in this series as they are published, you can make use of our standing order facility. To place a standing order please contact your bookseller or, in case of difficulty, write to us at the address below with your name and address and the name of the series. Please state with which title you wish to begin your standing order. (If you live outside the UK we may not have the rights for your area, in which case we will forward your order to the publisher concerned.)

Standing Order Service, Macmillan Distribution Ltd, Houndmills, Basingstoke, Hampshire, RG21 2XS, England.

Charlotte and Emily Brontë

Literary Lives

Tom Winnifrith

Senior Lecturer in English
University of Warwick

Edward Chitham

Senior Lecturer
The Polytechnic, Wolverhampton

MACMILLAN

First published 1989

Published by
THE MACMILLAN PRESS LTD
Houndmills, Basingstoke, Hampshire RG21 2XS
and London
Companies and representatives
throughout the world

Printed and bound in Great Britain at
The Camelot Press plc, Southampton

British Library Cataloguing in Publication Data
Winnifrith, Tom, *1938–*
    Charlotte and Emily Brontë : literary lives.
    — (Macmillan literary lives).
    1. Fiction in English. Brontë, Charlotte,
    1816–1855 & Brontë, Emily, 1818–1848
    I. Title   II. Chitham, Edward
    823'.8
    ISBN 0–333–42197–3
    ISBN 0–333–42198–1 Pbk

Contents

List of Abbreviations

BB	Branwell Brontë
BST	*Brontë Society Transactions*
CB	Charlotte Brontë
CH	Constantin Heger
EB	Emily Brontë
EN	Ellen Nussey
G	E. C. Gaskell, *The Life of Charlotte Brontë* (London, 1855)
PB	Patrick Brontë
SHCP	T. J. Winnifrith (ed.) *The Poems of Charlotte Brontë* (Oxford, 1984)
SHLL	T. J. Wise and J. A. Symington (eds) *The Brontës, Their Lives, Friendships and Correspondence* (Oxford, 1932)
WSW	W. S. Williams

1

Life

There is no shortage of books about the Brontës. The ready appeal of their novels to all ages in all ages, and the melancholy pathos of their lives have given rise to an abundance of critical and biographical studies. It is difficult to think of anything new to say about the Brontës, and this is perhaps one reason why wild speculation about the Brontës' lives and fantastic theories about their books have been all too prevalent. One of our objects has been to lay to rest some of the legends that have grown up around the inhabitants of Haworth parsonage. It is still commonly believed that Aunt Branwell was a cruel aunt, that Lowood in *Jane Eyre* was the exact image of Charlotte's and Emily's first school at Cowan Bridge, that various drunken characters in the novels are modelled on Branwell, that *Wuthering Heights* is the replica of a lonely farmhouse near Haworth, and that in her Belgian novels Charlotte shamelessly and artlessly wrote the diary of her experiences at the school of Monsieur and Madame Heger. Similarities have been found between some characters in the Brontës' lives and some characters in their works, but similarity is not identity, nor can, or should, we find real life models for all Brontë characters. No original for Heathcliff is going to spring from these pages.

In spite of being so frequently linked with the events of their authors' lives and Yorkshire background, the Brontë novels have a timeless quality about them and have appealed to many different countries and cultures. In teaching not only adolescents but mature students as well, not only from England but from all parts of the globe, we have found a regrettable but understandable ignorance about the world in which the Brontës lived and about which they wrote. The word Victorian is used, usually with contempt by our children, and sometimes with nostalgia by our contemporaries, to describe a world of stern strange fixed values, and this world is supposed to have existed far beyond Queen Victoria's reign from 1837 to 1901 to include any book written

1

between 1800 and 1960. It is insufficiently realised how many rapid changes in attitudes took place even in Queen Victoria's reign, and how often the Brontës who wrote in the early part of this reign challenged accepted attitudes of which they were sometimes not even aware. Religion and education figure prominently in the following pages which are about governesses who were daughters of a clergyman and who wrote books in which teachers and parsons figure prominently. Progressive attitudes to education, and the unwillingness or inability of modern churchmen to denounce sin, make the clergymen and teachers of the Brontë novels seem very odd, even though the Brontës are modern in denouncing some of their cruelties.

Our main source for knowledge of the Brontës, apart from the novels, is likely to be their correspondence, used as evidence by numerous biographers from Mrs Gaskell onwards. The fact that most of the Brontë letters that have survived were written by Charlotte, the fact that she wrote most of them to her rather dull and conventional friend, Ellen Nussey, and the fact that all letters, especially those written to Ellen Nussey, have been badly edited and inaccurately dated, have inevitably distorted our knowledge of the Brontës. In the notes we refer extensively to Mrs Gaskell and to her main modern successor, Winifred Gerin, authoress of biographies of all four Brontë children, but we must, at this stage, advise caution in using both these biographers. Mrs Gaskell had to be careful with Charlotte's husband and father breathing down her neck, while Mrs Gerin is insufficiently careful in linking fact and fiction.[1]

Apart from the novels and the letters, our knowledge of the Brontës is illuminated by the large amount of other writing that Charlotte, Branwell, Emily and Anne produced during their lifetime. This body of literature is inaccurately lumped together as the juvenilia, although Charlotte and Branwell were continuing to write prose stories, which have survived, well after their twenty-first birthdays, and Emily and Anne were writing both poetry, of which we have manuscripts, and prose, which has not survived, until the last years of their life. The juvenilia includes both poetry and prose. Some poems by the Brontë sisters were published in their lifetime, although these poems are but the tip of an iceberg. Some poems were originally composed as part of the two complicated prose sagas which, on the one hand Charlotte and Branwell, and on the other hand Emily and Anne, constructed and which played a major part in their imaginative life from childhood to adulthood. These two sagas are centred around the imaginary kingdoms of Angria for Branwell and Charlotte, and Gondal for Emily and Anne.

There are obvious dangers in using the juvenilia as evidence for what the Brontës thought. Extravagant claims have been made for their artistic merit, absurd parallels have been drawn between them and the mature novels, and biographical deductions have been drawn from material that has been badly edited and dated, and sometimes ascribed to the wrong Brontë. On the other hand it is clearly a mistake to ignore the juvenilia and poetry altogether. For Emily and Anne we have so little evidence that their poems must be taken into account. Some of Emily's poetry is of a very high quality. The immense and incoherent bulk of Charlotte's juvenilia, which has not yet been edited in a satisfactory fashion, does reveal her romantic fantasies and adolescent unhappiness more starkly than the prim letters to Ellen Nussey.[2]

Only perhaps in *Villette* do we find the exact balance between the unexciting world in which the Brontës lived their outward lives, where a call by a curate was a great event and a visit to a friend a great adventure, and the inner world of the imagination full of passion and privation and danger. One of the reasons why *Jane Eyre* and *Wuthering Heights* were thought so shocking when they were first published was that the people and events these novels described were so alien to the polite world of many of their readers, a world full of tea parties and mild gossip, much the same world as Anne Brontë describes at the beginning of *Wildfell Hall*. Branwell's drunken escapades and Charlotte's love affair with her teacher in Belgium, M. Heger, have been made to do heavy duty by people trying to make the lives of the Brontës as interesting as their books. The tragedy of the Brontës' early deaths is, of course, another source of interest, although such deaths were by no means rare in Victorian times. In a paradoxical way the most interesting thing about the lives of the Brontës is that they were so uninteresting.

It will be the task of the remainder of this chapter to summarise the story of these sad stunted lives while subsequent chapters, in a roughly chronological fashion, take particular aspects of these lives which are important for a study of their books. This is an account of Charlotte and Emily Brontë, but inevitably Branwell and Anne must feature. This is a literary life since, if the Brontës had written nothing, their history would be quite unremarkable. For a variety of reasons it is sometimes difficult to decide whether a knowledge of the Brontës' lives is more of a hindrance or a help in appreciating their books. The following account assumes that readers of the novels will want to know more about those who wrote them and the circumstances in which they were written.

Mr Brontë was born on 17 March 1777 in Northern Ireland. His origins were humble, but by his exertions he attracted the notice of powerful patrons who sent him to Cambridge. Here he took his degree, became ordained and after curacies in Essex and Shropshire, came to Yorkshire, a stronghold of the Evangelical Christianity which he always professed. In Yorkshire he met and married Maria Branwell in 1812, and in the next eight years she bore him five daughters and one son. Charlotte, Emily and Anne were born in 1816, 1818 and 1820 in the little village of Thornton, but in the year of Anne's birth the family moved to Haworth. This was in one sense a promotion as the parish was a large one, and one famous in Evangelical history, but conditions on the edge of the moor must have been rugged. Mrs Brontë did not live long to experience them, dying of cancer in 1821.

Mr Brontë made some rather pathetic efforts to remarry, but these came to nothing. Mrs Brontë's sister, Elizabeth, came from Cornwall to look after the children, and lived there until her death in 1842.

In 1824 the four elder girls were sent to school at Cowan Bridge, which was only 30 miles as the crow flies from Haworth though, given the difficulty of travel, the distance was a long one. The experiment was not a success as the two eldest girls, Maria and Elizabeth, fell ill and died. It is still open to doubt how far these deaths were due to the cruelty and incompetence of the school. Charlotte did suggest that the portrait of Lowood in *Jane Eyre* was based on Cowan Bridge, and that Maria Brontë was the model for Helen Burns. The identifications were denied after Charlotte's death by members of the family of William Carus Wilson, the proprietor of Cowan Bridge.

For over five years after being removed from Cowan Bridge in June 1825, Charlotte and Emily remained at home, being taught by their aunt. In June 1826, Mr Brontë brought home some wooden toy soldiers and this trivial gift to Branwell inspired the young children into writing a series of stories about them. Some of the early stories, written before the Brontës were into their teens, are naturally fairly rudimentary, but before Charlotte left for school in January 1831, she and Branwell were producing technically correct poetry and a variety of prose stories.

Charlotte went to school at Miss Wooler's establishment at Roe Head from January 1831 to May 1832. She met her two lifelong friends, Ellen Nussey and Mary Taylor, at this school and remained a friend of the headmistress, Margaret Wooler, for the whole of her life. From 1832 to 1835 all four Brontës were again at home and this was the time when the juvenile writings became something more than a childhood game for the children. Anne and Emily broke away from Charlotte and Branwell at some time between 1831 and 1834 to write their own saga about Gondal. Since only verse survives from this saga it is impossible to give an accurate account of what happened in it, nor is it likely that a coherent story would emerge. Gondal does seem, like *Wuthering Heights*, to have involved passion and savagery and, though set in an imaginary island of the Northern Pacific, the landscape of the poetry of Emily and Anne seems set in the same harsh and rugged Northern landscape which characterises both *Wuthering Heights* and *Wildfell Hall*.

Charlotte's and Branwell's writings about the kingdom of Angria survive, and we know more about it. Branwell seems to have taken the lead in a series of tales recounting the adventures of some English voyagers to West Africa. With a vague basis in fact, as the Brontës had read stories of travellers in Africa, the Angrian stories soon took on a fantastic colour with aristocratic houses and behaviour appearing in an improbable tropical setting. Some of the characters too began as historical personages, with the Duke of Wellington and his two sons, the Marquess of Douro and Lord Charles Wellesley, playing a large part, but gradually fiction took over. Douro became Charlotte's chief character, and the main focus of the Angrian stories and poems became the rivalry between him and Branwell's chief hero, Alexander Rogue, also known as Northangerland, just as Douro was known as Zamorna.

The writing of these adventures was interrupted by Charlotte going back, in May 1835 to Miss Wooler's school at Roe Head, this time as a teacher. She was accompanied first by Emily, but she did not last long, then by Anne who also became ill. Emily and Anne went as pupils. At some stage the school moved from Roe Head to Dewsbury Moor. Branwell made an unsuccessful attempt to become a portrait painter in London, probably in 1835, and

Emily was a teacher at Miss Patchett's school at Law Hill near
Halifax in the winter of 1838, after Charlotte had given up her
post at Roe Head. The Brontës were not happy as teachers but
there seemed few other prospects of employment open to them.
The writings of the Brontës at this time show this unhappiness.
Branwell was worried by the fact that his high literary and artistic
ambitions had come to nothing. Charlotte was disturbed at the
increasing gap between the wild world of her imaginary characters
and the humdrum reality of teaching her recalcitrant pupils. Anne
was touched by religious doubts, and Emily found it difficult to
survive away from home.

Charlotte received two proposals of marriage, one from Ellen
Nussey's brother in March 1839 and another in August 1840 from
a young Irish curate called Pryce. She refused both offers although,
apart from matrimony, few careers seemed open to her. An initial
venture as a governess to the Sidgwick family in 1839 proved
disastrous, and Anne was equally unsuccessful in the same year
in the house of Joshua Ingham of Blake Hall. Branwell's position
as tutor in the Postlethwaite family of Westmoreland in 1840 was
probably brought to an abrupt end by his being dismissed for
drunkenness. In 1840 Anne went as governess to the Robinsons
of Thorp Green where she was joined by Branwell in 1843.
Charlotte was again a governess from March to December 1841
with the Whites of Rawdon House whom she dismissed snobbishly as vulgar tradesmen, but with whom she got on rather better
than she had with the Sidgwicks.

In the intervals at home during these years as governesses, the
lives of the Brontës were enlivened by the presence in Haworth of
the Rev. William Weightman, their father's curate. He seems to
have been a pleasant, if flirtatious, young man. The evidence that
Anne fell in love with him is largely hypothetical, although it is
certainly impressive that Anne subsequently did not publish
much of her sad love poetry written during this time.[3] Emily's
poetry written during these years shows a continuing depth and
power, as she sternly questioned prevailing moral values.
Charlotte's prose stories were becoming more realistic. She also
received a discouraging reply from Southey in 1837 when she
asked his advice about literature, and Hartley Coleridge was not
much more helpful in 1840 when she sent him the manuscript of
Ashworth, a story with Angrian characters transmuted to a
Yorkshire setting, including some scenes set in a girls' school.

Branwell was also writing despondent poems and satirical stories at this time. He made an unsuccessful attempt to be a railway clerk, being dismissed for incompetence in 1842. The three sisters with encouragement from their father and aunt now planned to set up a school, and to this end Emily and Charlotte were sent to the Continent to improve their languages. The choice of Brussels in general and the Heger establishment in particular appears to have been largely fortuitous, although the presence of Mary Taylor in Belgium and the wish of the Brontës to learn German as well as French contributed towards this important decision.

Accompanied by their father, Emily and Charlotte arrived at the Pensionnat Heger on 15 February 1842. Both girls were in their twenties, but initially their position was very much that of school-girls. Their natural shyness, a foreign country and the alien faith of Catholic Belgium did not contribute to their happiness. But they had the company of each other, of the Taylors and their cousins the Dixons, and their stay was enlivened by the brilliant teaching of Monsieur Heger. The latter's influence on Charlotte's own emotional life is well known; his correction of the French exercises of Emily and Charlotte, a model to all teachers for diligence and sensitivity, had an important influence on the prose style of both sisters. Emily gained confidence in her ability, Charlotte learnt to prune extravagances.

At the end of 1842 the Brontës' stay in Belgium was darkened by a series of deaths. Mary Taylor's sister Martha died in October and was buried in Brussels. In Haworth first William Weightman and then Aunt Branwell fell ill and died. The girls hurried home but, in January, Charlotte returned alone to Brussels. The Hegers had promoted her to the post of teacher and initially Charlotte was happy. Mary Taylor was in Germany, but the Dixons were in Belgium, as were some other English acquaintances, the Wheelwrights, although both families left in the summer. Charlotte's friendship with Monsieur Heger ripened into love, and relations between Charlotte and both Hegers grew awkward. For much of the long vacation Charlotte was left on her own, a prey to the kind of loneliness and despair which beset Lucy Snowe in *Villette*, although it is a mistake to regard this novel, written nearly ten years later, as purely autobiographical. Charlotte did, like Lucy, visit the confessional.

On 1 January 1844 Charlotte returned to England. She found

Emily at home, while Anne and Branwell were apparently doing well at the Robinsons. Efforts to start a school proved fruitless. Letters to M. Heger reveal an increasing desperation. Emily may have been working on *Wuthering Heights* during this period. Anne had been writing a work entitled vaguely *Passages in the Life of An Individual*, which may be the same as *Agnes Grey*.[4]

In June 1845, Anne left her employment at the Robinsons saying that she had had a very unpleasant and undreamt-of experience of human nature.[5] Almost certainly this was the result of Branwell's conduct, although it is not clear exactly why Branwell was dismissed. He spread the story that there had been a love affair between him and Mrs Robinson. His sisters evidently believed this and adultery, hitherto treated in rather a cavalier fashion in the Brontë juvenilia, appears in a bad light in the published novels. For the remaining three years of his life Branwell was a constant source of anxiety to his family. A son who has given way to drink and drugs is still a source of shame in English families today. The middle of the nineteenth century was more charitable about drugs, though much less charitable about adultery and the possibility of eternal damnation. The fact that Branwell lived in a small village and that his father was the clergyman of that village must have added to the disgrace of his sensitive family.

Courage can quell despair: thus Charlotte in one of her less successful poems, and so it was that in the important years between 1845 and 1848, wracked by disappointment, ill health, anxiety and despair, the Brontë sisters produced two of the most famous of English novels. They were not helped by the men of the family, except perhaps indirectly. Hopes of founding a school faded at about the same time that it became clear that Branwell would never be in a position to support his sisters. Shortly afterwards Mr Brontë, approaching his seventieth birthday, showed increasing signs of blindness. Miraculously in August 1846, allegedly on the day Charlotte began *Jane Eyre*, Mr Brontë was operated on successfully for cataract.

With all his faults, Mr Brontë did provide a steady income for the Brontë household and a roof over their heads. The prospect of his death or permanent incapacity must have seemed appalling to the Brontë sisters, whose efforts to earn a living had not been conspicuously successful. We do not know if worry about their father's death was the spur to the Brontës' literary career, but it does not seem unlikely. Officially the occasion for the opening of this career was in the autumn of 1845 when Charlotte accidentally came across some of Emily's poems.

The discovery did not create immediate harmony in the Brontë household. Emily, according to Charlotte's account – written piously after a Victorian deathbed – was not pleased, and it took days to reconcile her to the possibility of publication. Emily was naturally displeased with intrusions into her thoughts and emotions. It is not clear how this displeasure manifested itself in the years between discovery and publication, especially as most signs of the displeasure were eradicated between the initial publication and the second edition published after Emily's death. Anne's contribution to the collected poems of the Brontës is unlikely to have been fully acknowledged in the light of Charlotte's patronising comments upon it. Charlotte appears to have taken control of efforts to publish the poems, but we do not know how far she took control of their editorship.

After the discovery of Emily's poems, publication proceeded rapidly. The Brontë sisters paid Aylott and Jones, a respectable firm of clerical publishers, the respectable sum of twenty-six pounds ten shillings, and *Poems by Acton, Currer and Ellis Bell* appeared, at the price of four shillings in May 1846. Though quite kindly reviewed, *Poems* only sold two copies. The poems selected had to have Gondal references eliminated from them, and with each sister contributing one poem in turn, Emily's powerful poetry was not adequately represented; but the complete failure of the poems is surprising.

Nothing daunted, the Brontës now tried approaching publishers with three prose stories. These were *Agnes Grey, Wuthering Heights* and *The Professor*, completed at the end of June 1846. For over a year the manuscripts went the rounds of various publishers, and were rejected by all of them. At some stage *The Professor* was separated from the other two novels and considered by a different set of publishers. Possibly Emily lengthened her novel in 1847 to make up for the omission. Charlotte is supposed to have begun *Jane Eyre* on the day of her father's eye operation in Manchester in August 1846. Thus, when *The Professor* was rejected by the firm of Smith Elder in July 1847, with a kindly and encouraging note that a work in three volumes would be acceptable, Charlotte was able to say that she had such a work in hand, and on 24 August sent off the manuscript.

George Smith at once saw its merits, agreed handsome terms

with Charlotte for the copyright, and *Jane Eyre* was published on 19 October 1847. Reviews were generally favourable, although there were comments on the coarseness of the work. By April 1848 the book had gone into a third edition. Meanwhile the firm of Thomas Newby and Son had accepted *Wuthering Heights* and *Agnes Grey* on much less favourable terms. Their publication was dilatory and unsatisfactory, but the novels eventually came out in December 1847. Reviewers were in general baffled by Emily's novel. It is not clear whether she ever embarked upon a second work; Anne had completed *Wildfell Hall* in time for it to be published in June 1848.

Newby had unscrupulously used the fact that the three sisters had published under the pseudonyms of Acton, Currer and Ellis Bell to suggest that the three authors were really one and the same person. It was to clear up this confusion that Anne and Charlotte visited Smith Elder in London during July 1848 where their appearance caused some surprise. The sisters still asked to keep their identity as authoresses a secret, and there was still confusion among reviewers who tended to lump the Bells together, seeing in them traits of brutality and coarseness.[6] The unfairness of these reviews hurt all three sisters, especially as their personal circumstances were very different from those the reviewers had imagined.

Branwell's health and morale had gradually deteriorated. Mrs Robinson's remarriage to a wealthy and titled widower must have destroyed any hopes he may have had after the death of her first husband. Debts pursued him, and he became incapable of looking after himself, nearly setting the house on fire on one occasion. His death on 24 September 1848 cannot have been wholly unexpected or even wholly unwelcome, but the Brontës had been a close knit family. Anne's health had always been delicate, but it was Emily who first became fatally ill, dying on 19 December 1848. Anne survived the winter precariously, with minor rallies occasionally giving some hope to her sister, but she too died at Scarborough on 28 May 1849.

Heroically Charlotte took up the novel which she had begun before her sisters' deaths. *Shirley* was completed at the end of August 1849 and published on 26 October. Inevitably the novel shows signs of the difficult circumstances in which it was written. The two heroines take on characteristics of Charlotte's two sisters, and in spite of the conventional happy ending, there is a sombre tone about the end of the book, for which we are not prepared by the satirical beginning. Although there were still attacks on the book's coarseness, reviewers were generally quite kind. After Emily's death Charlotte was not unwilling for her identity to be known, and reviewers may have been influenced by some knowledge of the writer's pathetic history.

As a famous authoress, Charlotte could have used her fame to make new friends, but shyness and depression made this difficult. She did pay several visits to the Smiths in London, and James Taylor, an employee of Smith, appears to have paid her a tepid courtship. Her relations with Smith himself are still a matter of conjecture. In the North of England she formed a difficult friendship with Harriet Martineau and a much more friendly link with Elizabeth Gaskell, her future biographer.

Charlotte found her next novel hard to write. Worry about it made her ill and confined her to Haworth. In 1850 she had prepared new editions of *Wuthering Heights* and *Agnes Grey*, together with a further selection of Emily and Anne's poems. She took considerable liberties with the text and her introduction to both Emily and Anne's work shows some lack of understanding, although her love for her sisters is clear.

The Professor was eventually published posthumously, but in 1851 Charlotte made another effort to get Smith Elder to accept it. Only when *The Professor* was finally rejected did she feel free to recast her Belgian material in the shape of *Villette*. Too much of this novel has been assumed to be autobiographical; not only is Monsieur Heger cast as Paul Emanuel, but George Smith is seen as John Bretton. James Taylor may have entered into the story which does owe something to Charlotte's loneliness in 1852 as well as her experiences in Belgium ten years earlier. The book cost Charlotte a great deal of anxiety, and her feeling of relief when the manuscript was dispatched and accepted in November 1852, before publication on 28 January 1853, augured ill for the success of any future novels.

Further writing was interrupted by the proposal on 13 December 1852 which Arthur Bell Nicholls, her father's curate, made to her. Initially Charlotte was hostile to this proposal, and her father even more so, but after leaving the village Mr Nicholls obtained permission to correspond with Charlotte, and gradually won his way. There is a gap in the correspondence with Ellen Nussey at this stage and Charlotte's change of mind is difficult to explain, although her loneliness and need to be loved have to be borne in mind. Charlotte was engaged in April 1854 and married on 29 July.

With her marriage Charlotte's literary career came to an end. Two fragments, *The Story of Willie Ellin* and *Emma*, begun in 1853, were not continued. Whether Mr Nicholls would have allowed her to continue writing is uncertain. He exercised censorship over Charlotte's correspondence with Ellen Nussey and seems to have enjoyed involving her in the humdrum duties of a clergyman's wife. Charlotte became ill in February 1855 with symptoms that look like morning sickness, but her pregnancy is not proven. She died on 31 March.

The Brontës lived through stirring times. The invention of the railway and the penny post created many changes in English life. Industrial advances and social reform proceeded apace. England was already, by the time of Charlotte's death, beginning to emerge as the greatest imperial power and workshop of the world. All these changes created all kinds of problems. Both changes and problems are only dimly reflected in the Brontës' novels which tend to be set in the time of previous generations and in spots remote from the industrial hub. A knowledge of contemporary England is useful for a study of the Brontës, but we must always remember how all the Brontës wilted when they were away from home. Other nineteenth-century authors can be compared to the Brontës, but the contrasts are obvious. It is dangerous to concentrate too much on Haworth and Yorkshire and the sad quiet life of Charlotte and Emily when looking at their strongly exciting works, but we cannot ever get away from this life entirely.

2

Origins

'The Celts', writes Phyllis Bentley, 'are fluent and fiery, restless and romantic, versatile and volatile, poetical and proud.' Dr Bentley has been only one of many writers to note a 'Celtic' tone in the work of the Brontës (and in their lives, especially those of Branwell and Emily). Elsie Harrison considered Northern Irish Methodism to be 'the clue to the Brontës'.[1] As the nineteenth century came to a close, a furious controversy about the origin of the Brontë genius erupted and has never finally subsided. All this might have been surprising to the original readers of *Jane Eyre*, or even the admiring public who welcomed Mrs Gaskell's *The Life of Charlotte Brontë*.

We may well think that generalisations about racial characteristics are fraught with danger and sinister overtones not suspected by the nineteenth-century proponents of the Celtic revival. Perhaps it may be as wrong as it is unscientific to point to the 'Celtic' origins of both Brontë parents as genetically ensuring that the family would be as they were. Yet there certainly do appear, as the lives of the Brontës unfold, characteristics which are habitually associated with those of 'Celtic' origin. The Brontës *were* fluent and they could be fiery; they *were* versatile, volatile and proud. Though it is only fair to point out that some of these characteristics are found in their heroes – Shelley, Byron, Coleridge and Southey – who were by no means all Celtic; yet the feeling that their genetic background does have some bearing on their temperament persists. There have been writers bold enough to claim that the Brontës owed all their success to their Irish ancestry; this may well be oversimplifying; the truth is perhaps less one-sided.

However, it is certainly worth noting that Yorkshire was an alien and distant environment for both the Brontë parents. Maria Branwell had been born near Penzance, into a respected Cornish family. For the short period during which her influence on her children was direct, before she died in 1821, she seems to have

13

been a steadying influence, expressing her moral values through the Wesleyan Methodist religion which she had brought with her. If her character could be said to be 'Celtic', perhaps this issued in an understanding of the part played by feeling in human life. Until her last illness she seems to have put up cheerfully with some 'eccentric' behaviour on the part of her husband. During her last few months on earth she became depressed and saddened: loyal to Mr Brontë but very unsure of what would happen to her unruly children after her death. She was small in stature, passing this characteristic on to all the children except Emily. Whether any of these characteristics can be described as 'Celtic' is debatable. Perhaps it was Anne who most took after her.

Probably it was Patrick Brontë who seemed the more Celtic to the nineteenth- and early twentieth-century biographers, and since it does seem that the value-system he acquired in his early years in Ireland deeply influenced the way the girls saw life, and there are even some hints that literary influence crossed the Irish Sea with him, it will be necessary to go into this background in some detail.

Patrick was born in Imdel, County Down, on 17 March 1777.[2] Both his name and his date of birth ensured that neither he nor his children would ever forget his Irishness. Early biographers who tried to discover more about the background were incredulous when they found that his birthplace was a little kiln cottage, where his father had roasted corn through the long nights, entertaining their neighbours to a host of traditional and other tales, acting and grimacing, lowering and raising his voice in the typical rhetorical devices of the Irish story-teller. The cottage was tiny; it had two rooms and, though kept spotlessly clean by Patrick's mother, there was really no room for the growing family. Patrick's father, Hugh, must have been hard-working since, in the course of time with economic success, they all moved to a two-storey house in Ballynaskeagh nearby. But the whole milieu was much too alien for the early biographers, who turned their backs firmly on it and concentrated on turning Charlotte into the respectable parson's daughter who finally made her way in the literary world of the mid-nineteenth century.

Yet Patrick caught his enthusiasms from Ireland, and transferred them to the children. We cannot really understand the way in which the Brontës grew up unless we appreciate the climate of social and artistic feeling in late eighteenth-century Ulster. Even

early commentators noted the sparseness of their material background: woollen clothes, the simple food, the general absence of
luxury. This aspect of their upbringing is only the obverse of the
very positive mania for the things of the mind, heart and spirit
which existed in the Brontë home. Further, though in some ways
it does not matter which side of the sectarian divide we place Mr
Brontë, since many of the values held were common to people on
both sides, it may be important to emphasise that as the child of a
Catholic mother and a virtual pagan, he was an outcast, who
lived with alienation and made his own terms with it. Thus Emily
learned not to mind being isolated from the rest of mankind, and
Charlotte almost expected misunderstanding. The whole family
learned to find contentment within themselves, rather than in
social esteem.

Patrick Brontë's father, Hugh Brunty, seems to have been an
Irish-speaking boy, who had grown up in the Boyne valley near
Drogheda, the very heart of the oldest Irish legends and customs.[3]
In his childhood he could see the tumuli that were dimly remembered by the natives to be the tombs of the Tara kings. Now
fairies lived in them, entering the narrow slits of doors at dead of
night. One was expected to leave saucers of milk out for them.
Hugh Brunty taught himself the legends and imbibed a keen
interest in politics, too. This he passed on to Patrick and his
brother, William, who subsequently took up the shillelagh and
fought at Ballynahinch in the 1798 revolution. Later, Emily used
some of this background in her Gondal stories and poems.

So story-telling was hereditary to Patrick Brontë and his four
brothers. They reverenced it. To them, the story was not an art
form that could be taken or left at will: it was their life-blood. It
quickly became the life-blood of the Brontë children. The power
of words had an almost supernatural aura, as we see in Charlotte's
juvenilia. Like Patrick, the Brontë children saw the pen and the
sword alike as mighty forces for changing the world. They did not
have modern eclectic notions about who were real Irishmen and
who were not. Thus they idolised the Duke of Wellington and
Dean Swift as well as Ossian.

Political debate was likewise important. It seems likely that
Hugh Brunty had used his rhetoric to propound rational but
revolutionary doctrines in 1798, and the whole family always felt
themselves involved in politics. Patrick sent out a stream of letters
to authorities aimed at changing things: among others, the state

of sanitation in Haworth, the type of guns used by British soldiers, the minds of local pastors. Rational but persuasive dispute was in the air at Haworth parsonage from the girls' childhood. So Charlotte writes in part to persuade; she has the missionary zeal. Anne, in particular, aims, like Swift, to 'vex' as well as entertain.

Patrick had been a weaver and blacksmith's boy before catching the eye of a Presbyterian minister and being put in charge of the Presbyterian school at Glascar. He threw his heart into education. He was very unlike the typical literary figure who takes on school teaching merely as a way of earning while establishing a public for his work. Patrick believed intensely in education. One can see this attitude in his determination to send his daughters to school to extend their knowledge. He had an enlightened, positive view of it. He also thought that girls should be taught as much as boys. This seems unusual for the day in which he lived, and we must put down to Patrick's lack of what would now be called 'sexism' the freedom to write and imagine that the girls had. There are stories of his pleading with local farmers in County Down to let girls stay on at school, not become slaves to the sink. Though in the event, Charlotte, Emily and Anne all swept the house and cut up the stew in the kitchen, they did not spend all their time doing these things. As the boy of the family, Branwell was still favoured, but among the nest of young writers in the parlour and the kitchen, he had to make his own way. There was never any suggestion that education was unsuitable for girls. Charlotte specialised in French, Emily in German, but Anne was not prevented from learning Latin, just as Branwell had done. Though Branwell was considered the family hope in the early days, there seem to have been no hindrances placed in the way of the girls running wild on the moors, writing away in the dusk till their eyes failed, and discussing politics or generalship. Mr Brontë did not seem to understand that these were unusual pursuits for girls; he had evidently formed his own opinion of the potential of girls by teaching them in the school at Glascar.

Part of Mr Brontë's heritage was a lively view of the world to come. Orthodox Christian beliefs did not cover all the possible attitudes of the Ulster peasants towards what might happen once we have left this life. Mr Brontë's brothers loved to tell ghost stories, in part derived from popular ballads, no doubt. The evidence suggests that they sometimes satirised the credulity of the people, but that they half-believed their own horrific yarns. In part they persuaded themselves of the truth of their own imaginations: the trait remained strong in all the Brontë children. Ellen Nussey recalled Charlotte scaring a dormitory full of girls at Roe Head with horrific tales, and she was later herself terrified by Mr Brontë's own horrific tales, told with every rhetorical device, in the parsonage kitchen. Thus supernatural agencies are present in all the Brontë novels, appearing in both trivial and weighty contexts. Jane Eyre hears the voice of Rochester through telepathy; Heathcliff sees Catherine's shadowy presence; there are grey ghosts in the yard in *Villette*. These represent the Brontë's intense half-beliefs. They are not added to the novels because the girls had read Gothic tales: they are direct imports from the tradition across the sea bolstered, doubtless, by the stories told by the old servant, Tabitha Aykroyd. Soon the family were to be put to the test. They were to lose their mother and dear elder sisters. Would their belief in ghosts stand up to this? It did so; Emily was never free of the haunting figures of Maria and Elizabeth, developing throughout her life into stranger and stranger figures of alternate love and revenge.

The town of Penzance, from which the Branwell family hailed, was already in the late eighteenth century a centre of Wesleyanism. It is important here to note that there has been a confusion by some previous writers on the Brontës between Methodism and Calvinism. Wesleyans were not Calvinists, and in fact a strenuous dispute was taking place between the two groups over a point very similar to the one which Anne Brontë was to stress in such poems as 'A Word to the Elect' and in *Wildfell Hall*. Put very crudely, the argument was between those who believed that only 'the elect' were predestined for salvation, and those who thought salvation could be for all. Maria Branwell, brought up in the Wesleyan tradition, must have held the latter view: 'that Jesus had died "for all"' (though this did not mean that all would respond to his action). Her sister Elizabeth was also a Wesleyan, and we cannot ascribe the hatred of the Brontë girls for Calvinism to some form of rebellion against their aunt. More likely, their aunt and Maria Branwell had joined forces with their father and condemned Calvinism, and the three novelists were simply arguing further along the same lines.

The Branwells were a much respected family in Penzance, where one of Maria's brothers, Benjamin, was mayor of the town in 1809. Thus the Brontës were certainly aware of differences of social background: their mother's origins were bourgeois (despite an ultimate background in piracy, or so it was alleged), while their father hailed from the Irish peasantry. Not a great deal can be learnt about the attitudes of Charlotte and the others to their Cornish relatives; a cousin visited her after the deaths of Branwell, Emily and Anne, in 1851, but she says little about him. Despite her alleged dislike of Haworth and the North, Aunt Elizabeth dutifully remained with the girls until her death, and perhaps found her greater independence at a distance from the close-knit family in Cornwall a precious freedom.

When the six Brontës were very young, Miss Branwell had certainly done her best to introduce them into society. Visits seem to have been made to various neighbouring families in Haworth and Keighley, though the Brontë children appear to have been very reserved and to have preferred playing their own games among themselves. Mrs Gaskell told several stories of the shyness of the Brontë girls when in company. Nevertheless, the impressions gained at this time about social manners and customs may have played a part when Charlotte came to write about life at Thornfield. The socialisation process failed, but Charlotte's sharp eyes and capacious memory stored details of the fractious children and partial servants, and these impressions seem to have been integrated into her later writing.

It is also important to note that Maria Branwell, the mother of the Brontës, was as actively committed to a religious outlook on life as their father. She placed a spiritual dimension at the forefront of their early upbringing. Soon the eldest girl, named after her mother, was leading the other five in prayers and Bible reading, a foundation without which the Brontës could not have written as they did, and about which more will need to be said later. It is vital to note that before any disaster had struck the young family, before even their mother had died in so untimely a fashion, they were all aware that this life was transitory and impermanent, and that reality was beyond. Things unseen were more potent than things seen, even when they were children. This is an underlying factor in all the Brontë novels and most of the poetry. Branwell might react against it, and Emily interpret it in her own way, but all of them had imbibed this inescapable view literally at their mother's knee. Ultimately, the passages on the pains of hell in *Wildfell Hall*, the ghostly presence in the red room in *Jane Eyre*, and the powerful Platonism of some of Emily's later poems, as well as the whole ambience of *Wuthering Heights*, are all traceable to these childhood influences.[4]

A number of writers have tried to discover Methodist influence in the area of County Down where Patrick Brontë grew up. John Wesley had indeed travelled there, and was welcomed in churches and meeting houses. But it seems more likely that the Methodist strand of the Brontë's upbringing should be ascribed to the Branwell side of the family. Maria Branwell wrote a number of letters to Patrick, some of which have been preserved. Their tone is earnest, though humorous in places. From them we can see that the mother of the Brontës was no cypher. Coming from a rather higher social stratum than Patrick, she appears to have been attracted by his charm and fluency, his eager enthusiasm, and perhaps some of the very outlandishness which he passed on to his daughters.

To her and her sister Elizabeth, who came to look after the children when their mother died, we may probably ascribe part of Charlotte's snobbery and concern for social advancement. This concern sometimes seems ill-matched with the gaucheness of the girls, and is hardly noticeable in the case of Emily, whose painful shyness cut her off from almost all social contacts. Their Aunt Elizabeth had certainly tried to inculcate some graciousness into them but she was not always very successful in this, even when they were children. The diary papers left by Emily and Anne record cases of Aunt Elizabeth being cheeked and flouted, though Charlotte always spoke highly of the organisation she introduced into their potentially chaotic lives.

Assessment of Aunt Elizabeth's character has always been hard. The servants thought she was a tartar, but she was not cruel or vindictive, though possibly her discipline may have been very firm at times. She does not seem to be a prototype for Aunt Reid in *Jane Eyre*. The glimpses of her which are found in letters and other material show her as chatty, sociable and generous, if determined.[5]

The Brontës' work is firmly rooted in Northern England. Had their parents continued to live in Ireland or Cornwall, this could not have been the case. The third local influence on the family is the West Riding of Yorkshire. As soon as the novels had been first read, critics began to describe them in terms of provinciality. The scenes and societies portrayed were very un-metropolitan, and there were only slight or disparaging references to the South of England. This provincial viewpoint of the Brontës was not a conscious choice, though it was later consciously endorsed. The Brontës wrote of the North because they were naturalised in the North, rooted as firmly as any wiry heather plant.

Mrs Gaskell began her great biography with a description of the West Riding, Haworth in particular. She contrasted it with the rest of England, even Lancashire. But perhaps the true contrast is between Pennine country and the rest. Even at school in Cowan Bridge (Lancashire) the Brontës were in a Pennine valley. Even on holiday at Hathersage, Derbyshire, in 1845 Charlotte was in a Pennine village. When Emily went to Law Hill, she was living on a Pennine eminence. Mrs Gaskell wrote much of her work in Manchester, but she had approached it from the Cheshire plains, and the North Country as she experienced it in Cheshire was not the North of the Pennine West Riding.

Mr Brontë never precisely flourished in Yorkshire, but he subsisted without friction because there seems to have been something in his independent temperament that won respect from his parishioners, whether at Hartshead, where the eldest children were born, or Thornton, or at Haworth, where he succeeded in overcoming a cool reception and became quietly trusted by the villagers. (It is alleged that the crucial point in Mr Brontë's favour, according to a parishioner, was that 'he minds his own business'.) The Brontës were never intimate with the villagers. Branwell learnt his way to the Black Bull Inn, but some of his exhibitionism there may have been due to the very fact that he was not a native. Charlotte taught in the Sunday school, but she gained a reputation as a hard mistress, who did not seem to have the knack of attaching her scholars to herself with affection. Emily seems to have passed through the village in a dream, though Charlotte noted the sharp eyes that took in the appearance of the village people. She might equally have noted Emily's sharp *ears* which recorded the Haworth dialect impeccably.

The young Brontës' experience began in Thornton, a village nearer to Bradford and less exposed to wind and rain than Haworth. But it does share many characteristics with their later home and deserves some notice. Its pastures and meadowland, as well as its church and village houses, have left their mark on the novels.

At Thornton the Brontës would first learn about the solidity and firmness of Pennine stone. As at Haworth later, their house was of stone, a sturdy building that might have aspects of castle or prison. The Brontës' enthusiasm for stories involving prisons may have originated in the high-walled yard at Thornton, if not in the Haworth cellars. Charlotte retained distant memories of Thornton all her life, with her mother nursing Branwell on her knee. Near the house were closes of pasture where sheep grazed (in Charlotte's revisions of Emily's poems these were sometimes romanticised into deer). Mr Brontë loved to take the children on rambling walks in the neighbourhood, the smallest being led along by the elders, or carried on his shoulder. The children were very often out of doors in all kinds of weather. Emily's soft rains, cloudy evenings, calm summer mornings and thundery nights began to be observed here. The scents of Rochester's flower garden were first appreciated by Charlotte at Thornton, perhaps at the house of Elizabeth Firth, Kipping, where the children were welcome guests.[6]

It is perhaps rightly assumed that the name Thornfield in *Jane Eyre* has an obvious allusive meaning. But it may be too that the house takes its name in part from Charlotte's first home. The observation of the natural scene begun here comes to fruition in the novel. For example, there is the well known passage in which, one still January, Jane takes a letter to the post at Hay. The walk is to be interrupted suddenly by the startling arrival of Rochester, who symbolically falls from his Byronic/Romantic horse. The description of the lane is brilliantly evocative of the English countryside in January. It is three o'clock in the afternoon, and the church bell tolls the hour; the bell may be a combination of Haworth old clock and the bell at the 'Bell Chapel'. Jane praises the solitude of the lane to Hay, which she recalls in summer with its roses and in autumn with its hazel nuts. There are now only hips and haws in the hedgerows, and the 'little brown birds, which .... looked like single russet leaves that had forgotten to drop'.

It is impossible to say exactly when first Charlotte began to observe the landscape in this way. Some elements in her description must derive from the attempts by the children to capture landscapes in drawing; Bewick has his effect. But the colours are bright and clear; they must be observed in nature, and the observation is likely to have begun at Thornton. After the description of the scene in the lane, Jane turns to look down at Thornfield, where she notes its grey battlements, the woods and rookery: details observed by Charlotte in a variety of West Yorkshire contexts. The country round Thornfield is softer than the Haworth moors, but it might well be Yorkshire scenery.[7]

It was at Thornton that the children learnt that their father's business was to attend to the work of God in the area. This included visiting and counselling the villagers, taking Sunday services, and supervising the renovations on the Bell Chapel, which Mr Brontë 'beautified'. Later, Charlotte is reported to have had 'eyes that looked through you'. From her childhood days, she studied people with an intensity they found disconcerting. Thornton villagers would find themselves being stared at and annotated. During those very early years, Charlotte seems to have been building up a picture of domestic humanity which underpins the exotic or Romantic elements of her novels.

Nevertheless, the move to Haworth was crucial for the development of the family's authorial skills. In particular, it is hard to see how Emily could have written *Wuthering Heights* if her life had been passed mainly at Thornton. Access to the wild moors is harder from there, and there are more trees and meadows. So it was a portentous day when, in 1820, the Brontë family moved house, in a convoy of farm carts, over the hills to Haworth.

Though the Brontë novels have such a strong aura of place about them, no recognisable features of Haworth village itself appear in them. The steep main street, culminating in a wider space with shops, post office and public houses, is unique, but it does not play any part in *Jane Eyre* or *Wuthering Heights*. The stretch of moorland extending to Ponden and Stanbury blends with Halifax to form the setting for Emily's novel. One might have expected more small detail to be drawn from Haworth itself, but this is not so. Nevertheless, Haworth village provides the local base on which all the Brontë novels set in England are built. The Brontës had a sense of belonging to Haworth; the sense of belonging that many Brontë characters exhibit is related to this fact.

The one clear exception to this neglect of Haworth is the case of the church building and churchyard. Emily writes in her poems of the 'old church' or the 'minster' and in one poem the church clock is mentioned. Living next to an ancient graveyard certainly had an effect on her, and she thought a great deal about the problems of reconciling the heaven she had been told of where her sisters Maria and Elizabeth were said to be, and the bodies buried in such close proximity to her house by John Brown, the Haworth sexton.

Mrs Gaskell was, of course, immensely impressed by the desolate location of Haworth and felt that its isolation was at least in part responsible for the Brontës' development. Her own sketch of the church and parsonage should be studied to appreciate how she viewed Charlotte's background. The house itself, in Mrs Gaskell's drawing, seems gaunt and Gothic: it is, of course, not so at all, being a perfectly conventional late eighteenth-century building.

The churchyard also seems rough and the neighbouring buildings towering and misshapen; the moors loom above in the distance. Comparison of this sketch with the real scene will show how Mrs Gaskell saw Charlotte and the others, and illustrates the way in which she has influenced later opinion. In reality, Haworth was certainly isolated on the western side, but the church was not desolate and the parsonage homely, not lowering.

It seems quite likely that 'polite' society was to some extent lacking in the vicinity, but all contact with other humans was not interrupted by the Brontë's move. We should not overlook the close relationship the girls seem to have established with the servants, the Browns, Tabitha Aykroyd, and various other local contacts. After the sisters' deaths, local people apparently held the opinion that they did not mix much in society and avoided contact with the village. This was only partly true at any time, and less so during their childhood. It is well known that Charlotte and Anne both taught in the Sunday school as they grew older. The villagers' impression was that Charlotte was a hard taskmistress, but not an absentee. From these contacts, the Brontës derived knowledge of less exalted people; the realism of the servants in *Wuthering Heights* perhaps depends on them. Emily's acute ear for the dialect likely to be used by Joseph was being trained from her very earliest childhood.

As the young Brontës grew up and became more adventurous, their wanderings across the moors between Haworth and Ponden extended. One crucial event may have been the Crow Hill bog burst of September 1824, when a storm struck the moorland and released torrents of water which had been building up beneath the surface of the bog due to heavy rain in the previous week. Mr Brontë watched anxiously from the parsonage windows, for Emily,

Branwell and Anne were caught in it as a tide of mud and rocks came surging downhill to end on the flat space near Ponden Hall. It is not sure how the servant was able to protect her charges that afternoon; Mr Brontë saw the whole episode as a sign from heaven. It is likely that Emily felt exhilarated rather than terrified by this show of natural power.[8]

It could have been on that afternoon that the family was introduced to the residents of Ponden Hall, where one of Mr Brontë's church trustees, Robert Heaton, lived. The date of renovations at Ponden, 1801, appears early in *Wuthering Heights* and suggested to early commentators that Ponden had been a major influence on the novel. It is certain that Emily, Anne and Branwell used to visit the hall; their use of the well-stocked library will be dealt with later.

It used to be thought that Ponden had been the 'original' of Thrushcross Grange. That may not quite be the case, but it did contribute more than a date above a door. It seems probable that Emily formed a habit of crossing the moorland to Ponden, often with Anne, and she may have spent a considerable amount of time as a young girl reading in the library. (It is also possible that she heard of some old tragedies there.) It is featured strongly in the novel, and also occurs as a background in one of Emily's French *devoirs*, produced while she was in Belgium in 1842. But the park at Thrushcross does not correspond to anything at Ponden; the origins of that seem to be at Halifax, where Emily lived for six months during 1838–39.

There were many isolated farms on the moorland to the west of Haworth. While Charlotte was away at school in 1831 and 1832, Emily and Anne may well have explored these remote places. The location of one, Top Withens, has seemed to many commentators to correspond with that of Wuthering Heights, but there is no evidence to support this guess and, in fact, the farm, now only a ruin, was never much like the castellated mansion described in the novel. Even its situation does not seem to match very closely the situation of the Heights, despite the similarity in name. There seems to be a much better candidate for the original of Wuthering Heights in the shape of High Sunderland Hall at Halifax.

Meanwhile Charlotte was returning to her father's earlier haunts and was near the birthplace of her older sisters when she went to school at Roe Head. Not far from here, Mr Brontë had taken a strongly individual line in the struggle between workmen and woollen merchants. This industrial background was to be used by Charlotte in *Shirley*. It is likely she began to make contact with it during these years, as a young teenager. Her association with Roe Head, and the Miss Woolers who ran it, was never placid, but it did give her confidence in talking to strangers which Emily never attained.

As an instance of what has been said regarding the influence of early background upon the Brontës' mature work, it might be worth taking a short passage from *Wuthering Heights* in order to trace the deepest layers of the novel. We shall select the end of Chapter V, the passage in which old Mr Earnshaw dies. Earnshaw died, we are told, 'one October evening', when 'a high wind blustered round the house, and roared in the chimney; it sounded wild and stormy, yet it was not cold.' The month is given, though 'winter', 'autumn' or no word at all would have been quite acceptable. Emily is specific about days and months, as she learnt from her father's need to know the Church calendar, printed at the beginning of prayer books. This calendar, with its 'golden days' and moons, would be read by Emily as she sat in church each Sunday. The accurate weather observation, too, is that of a country household, and the wind is roaring in the parsonage chimney.

Meanwhile Joseph is reading his Bible and Earnshaw stroking Cathy's 'bonny hair'. The action may be that of Mr Brontë; the word 'bonny' is both Yorkshire and Ulster. Cathy sings her dozing father to rest: a permanent rest, as he is on the point of death, though no one realises this. 'She began singing very low . . .' So Cathy, like Emily and the other Brontës, has the traditional unselfconscious attitude to singing common in folk cultures. In his youth, Mr Brontë is reputed to have been a ballad singer; it is likely that this tradition was reinforced by the Haworth servants. The Bible reading of Joseph might originate from either parent or both: the Bible reading habit would have been part of Emily's earliest memories. Half an hour later, it is discovered that old Earnshaw is dead; Catherine screams out, and 'they both set up a heart-breaking cry'. Nelly joins with them, and the three howl 'loud and bitter'. Such howling at the death of a relative is recorded in Mr Brontë's novel *The Maid of Killarney* as 'keening'. Joseph, the Calvinist, hushes them. Emily had already explored the conflict between sorrow and delight in a saint's transfer to heaven in 'Shed no tears o'er that tomb', written several years before the novel.

When Earnshaw's death is realised, Nelly travels, through 'wind and rain' to Gimmerton for the doctor and parson. Emily shows her disrespect for the latter by pointedly noting that he 'said he would come in the morning'. Both the Ulster tradition of her father and her mother's Methodism, might tend to see the establishment parson as disinclined to leave his bed at night for a death. After returning through the Yorkshire autumn rain, Nelly goes to see the children, Cathy and Heathcliff. 'The little souls were comforting each other with better thoughts than I could have hit on; no parson in the world ever pictured heaven so beautifully as they did, in their innocent talk . . .' Despite the initial wailing, the two 'innocents' (the subsequently wicked Heathcliff is one) are picturing heaven vividly, in the manner of the strong tradition handed down to the young Brontës by both parents. Eyes are turned heavenwards, and Nelly now emphasises this craving for the life beyond death with her 'I could not help wishing we were all safe there together'.

Like so much of *Wuthering Heights*, this section is redolent of childhood associations, going back to parental example. We note also the sharp audial sense, shown in the speech rhythms, for example, the second person singular of 'Why canst thou not always be a good lass, Cathy?' The description, too, is direct, almost balladic: 'The poor thing discovered her loss directly – she screamed out –' (Note unconventional punctuation.) In such ways and more, the mature Brontë novels and poetry return to their roots, to the impressions gathered by the sisters in childhood.

The three geographical areas of the British Isles with which the Brontës felt themselves to be associated, all had a permanent and crucial effect on their finished writings. Without the Irish background, it is unlikely that *Wuthering Heights* would have obtained its flavour of oral saga, of deeply felt family history, and some at least of its supernatural elements. Nature in the magic territory of the heights is animated, like the fields and raths of Northern Ireland in the eighteenth century. *Jane Eyre* draws some of its warmth and drama from the Pennine isolation of Haworth, Cowan Bridge and Thornton. The stone battlements of Thornfield are solid Pennine rock, just as much as Heathcliff is 'whinstone'. *Wildfell Hall* exhibits the serious purpose of Wesleyanism, passed down from their Cornish mother and aunt to the whole family, and taken particularly to heart by Anne.

What the Brontës might have produced if Patrick had remained in his first curacy among the gentler hills of Shropshire, or if he had married Mary Burder from Essex, we shall never know. It is most unlikely that they would have written the Brontë novels and poetry as we know them.

3

Religion

Religion is a sensitive subject. People argued fiercely in the nineteenth century on religious matters, as they argue fiercely now, with the difference that the Victorian age had different topics to dispute and more actively religious people to dispute them. Our present concern about the ordination of women or the literal truth of the virgin birth would have shocked our great grandparents. On the other hand we live in an age where some attempts have been made to bridge the gap between both the Non-conformists and the Anglican Church, and the Anglican Church and the Roman Catholics; we are therefore amazed to find in the nineteenth century not only a vast chasm between these three main divisions of Christianity, but terrible disputes within them.

Only perhaps in Northern Ireland does religious feeling run so high today, and it was appropriately, if confusingly, from Northern Ireland that Mr Brontë came. His ancestry was probably Catholic, his upbringing Non-conformist, but it was a clergyman of the Church of England that Mr Brontë became, after travelling to Cambridge to read his degree, at that time a necessary qualification for ordination as an Anglican priest. It is a mistake to view eighteenth-century Ireland in twentieth-century terms, since the rebellion of Wolfe Tone in 1798, in which Mr Brontë's brother took part, was a revolt of Catholic and Non-conformist alike against the Anglican establishment, but hostility to Catholics in Northern Ireland remains a regrettable feature of both centuries, and this hostility, masking his own antecedents, was something that Mr Brontë passed on to his children. Even in England anti-Catholic feeling was rife, being particularly virulent around 1829, at the time of the Catholic Emancipation Act, and around 1845, at the time of the defection of Newman to Rome. Emily and Charlotte experienced Catholicism in Belgium and disliked it; the hostility of Charlotte, compounded by loneliness and homesickness, makes itself felt in her novels.

The gap between the Church of England and the Non-conformists is harder to explain, since in the person of John Wesley, the founder of the Methodist movement, who lived from 1703 to 1791, we have someone who tried to bridge it. Wesley was an ordained minister of the Church of England and was responsible more than any other man for that greater seriousness in religion with a strong emphasis on good works, upright behaviour and a belief in the Bible, which we have come to know as the Evangelical movement. This movement was dominant in the Church of England in the first quarter of the nineteenth century. Mr Brontë was an Evangelical and, in many ways, his daughters inherited his beliefs. Unfortunately Wesley was not content to remain within the confines of the Anglican Church, to which he had made such an important contribution, but instead, by ordaining his own ministers, he virtually founded a separate religious sect, known as Wesleyans or Methodists. These, like the older Non-conformist movements, such as the Presbyterians and Baptists, refused to accept the authority of the Anglican bishops on doctrine or Church organisation and, as we find at Haworth, members of these churches were reluctant to subsidise the Church of England by paying church rates.

The Wesleyans were strong in the industrial parts of England, where their simple message brought hope to the working class. Although the English Labour Party is supposed to owe more to Methodism than to Marxism, and both Methodists and Evangelicals showed a praiseworthy wish to better the lot of the urban poor, the leaders of both Church parties were conservative rather than radical. On the other hand, as Charlotte Brontë shows in *Shirley*, the Methodist movement did also attract some extreme revolutionaries anxious to overthrow the government and destroy the power of the capitalist factory owners. Doctrinal rather than political differences were more serious obstacles to unity and indeed, after Wesley's death, the Methodists split into different factions. Even in his lifetime Wesley quarrelled with his chief lieutenant, George Whitfield, over the issue of Calvinism. Whitfield, like many people inside and outside the Church of England, followed the doctrine of John Calvin that people were pre-ordained to salvation and damnation. Such a belief, although it follows logically enough from thinking of the Deity as both omnipotent and omnisicient, leads to unpleasant feelings of despair if one thinks one is damned, and sanctimoniousness if one thinks one is saved. All the Brontë children appear to have felt the despair and despised the sanctimoniousness.

Calvinism, though frequently confused with Methodism, is not the same as it; Aunt Branwell was a Methodist, but there is no evidence that she was a Calvinist. Mr Brontë's predecessor at Haworth, the famous William Grimshaw, was a Calvinist although, unlike Wesley, he remained faithful to the Church of England. There is no evidence for Mr Brontë himself preaching Calvinistic doctrines, although his sermons, letters, stories and poems are full of references to Hell and damnation. It now seems embarrassing for almost any religious sect to mention, let alone believe in, eternal punishment for sinners, but in the middle of the nineteenth century almost everyone believed in a literal hell. It is greatly to the credit of the Brontë sisters, perhaps influenced by the awful example of their brother dying as a drunkard and an adulterer, that they seemed to have had serious doubts about eternal damnation.

The reaction of the Brontës against strict Evangelicanism was in keeping with the spirit of the age. By the middle of the century both Methodism and the Evangelical movement had lost much of their vigour. In the 1840s the most exciting and controversial views in the Church of England were those held by Newman and his followers. Known variously as the Oxford movement, because so many of its leaders were connected with that university, or Tractarians, because of Newman's famous tracts stating his position, or Anglo-Catholics because of their similarity in doctrine to the Roman Catholics, or Puseyites because of another leader, Charles Pusey, who unlike Newman did not go over to Rome, they are perhaps best called High Churchmen to distinguish them from the Evangelical Low Church. They placed great emphasis on the rituals and ceremonies of the church, and were less devoted to the Bible.

Deriving some of its inspiration from the Romantic movement, the Oxford movement might have attracted the romantic minds of the Brontës, and Charlotte Brontë's often expressed antipathy to Romish ritual and superstition perhaps conceals a secret attraction to it. On the other hand, she had not been impressed by the High Church curates she met in Haworth and satirised them mercilessly in *Shirley*. Mr Nicholls was a High Churchman, although it is hard to find anything specifically High Church in his views except a general dislike of dissenters. In this he was joined by the only other curate to have made much impression upon the Brontës, the Rev. William Weightman. He is supposed to have been the model for Mr Weston in Anne Brontë's *Agnes Grey*, but there is little evidence for this. The other clergyman in this novel, Mr Hatfield, has certain High Church features, 'his favourite subjects being church discipline, rites and ceremonies, apostolical succession, the duty of reverence and obedience to the clergy, the atrocious criminality of dissent, etc.',[1] but oddly the same character gabbles through the service in a way that is hardly in keeping with High Church pretentions or practice. Hypocrisy and a general unwillingness to match deeds to words was something that the Brontës found as a shared feature of the extremes of High and Low Church, although their accusations may have lacked substance.

Temperamentally the Brontës were probably closest to the third great division of the Church of England in the nineteenth century, the Broad Church. This movement achieved its greatest prominence after the Brontës had died with, for instance, the publication in 1860 of *Essays and Reviews*, in which a group of Broad Churchmen adopted a liberal attitude to the literal truth of the Bible, thus arousing the anger of the still strong Evangelical party. Earlier, under such leaders as Thomas Arnold, they had quarrelled with the Tractarians over Church discipline. Arnold had died in 1842, but through his headmastership of Rugby School continued to exercise immense influence after his death, as pupils and teachers from this school rose to positions of authority in other schools and in the Church. Charlotte met the Arnold family in Westmoreland in the last years of her life. Both in her letters and in her novels she appears to approve of the Broad Church's tolerance and insistence on good conduct as the principal feature of Christianity. Mr Weston in *Agnes Grey* is a somewhat shadowy figure, but in his comforting of Nancy Brown he takes a Broad Church line.

Just as it is hard at times to distinguish the Low Church from Methodism or the High Church from Roman Catholicism, so the Broad Church at times in the eyes of its enemies came perilously close to agnosticism or atheism. There were sects which by appearing to deny a central part of the Christian creed were almost reckoned to be outside the pale. The Unitarians were such a sect, since they did not believe in the Trinity, but Charlotte had no difficulty in making friends with the Unitarian Mrs Gaskell.

She also was friendly for a time with Harriet Martineau, whose brother James was a celebrated Unitarian thinker, but Harriet Martineau's position eventually became too agnostic for Charlotte to stomach. Anne Brontë corresponded with the Rev. David Thom, the leader of a small sect known as the Universalists, who did not believe in the eternity of damnation, but rather in universal salvation for all. When the Rev. Frederick Maurice preached these doctrines in 1853, he was dismissed from his post at King's College, London; Charlotte sympathised with him. It must be remembered that in the middle of the century it was almost impossible for anyone in public life to express atheistical or agnostic views, and it was fairly dangerous to state unorthodox sentiments.[2]

Oddly, two of the Brontë children are thought to be unbelievers. Branwell, though a friend of William Weightman until his death in 1842, and a friend of the sexton, John Brown, until his own death, was uttering unorthodox sentiments in his poetry as early as the 1830s, and his prose stories contain some savage satires against religion, although usually the form of worship so satirised was extreme Non-conformism, also held up to scorn by his sisters. His lapse into drunkenness and his affair, real or imagined, with Mrs Robinson, were clearly sins in the eyes of most religious sects, and especially grievous to Evangelicals, just as his consequent despair must have caused grave alarm to his family, who were comforted by thoughts of a death-bed repentance. It is customary to blame religion for Branwell's decline, his Calvinist fears that he was already damned being thought of as an excuse for the readiness with which he was prepared to damn himself still further. In addition Branwell's sensitivity to hypocrisy may have rendered him hostile to the religion he saw preached but not practised. Mr Robinson was a clergyman, although he did not seem to have been an active one, and his library was full of Evangelical tracts. But Anne Brontë lived in the same household and preserved her religious faith, although her rather morbid poetry is not as powerful as that of some of her brother's despairing sonnets.

Emily's religious views are also assumed to be unorthodox on the evidence of her poetry and of *Wuthering Heights*. In her novel there is little mention of the clergy apart from the curate who soon despairs of teaching the unruly young Earnshaws, but Joseph's evangelical piety is keenly satirised and Nelly Dean's more conventional piety is more gently mocked. Such lines in Emily's poetry as:

> Vain are the thousand creeds
> That move men's hearts, unutterably vain
> Worthless as withered weeds
> Or idlest froth amidst the boundless main[3]

seem to reflect a total contempt for the many and varied forms of religious belief that we have been describing, and there is much to commend in the suggestion that much of Anne Brontë's writing in the last years of her life was devoted to the contradiction of her sister's atheistical doctrines.

Yet beyond the fact that Emily, unlike Charlotte or Anne, did not teach in Sunday school, possibly because of her antipathy to the role of teacher, there is almost no evidence for Emily rebelling against the conventional practice of religion which, in an Evangelical clergyman's household, went far beyond going to church every Sunday. It is true that we have precious little evidence of anything in Emily's life, and strangely little about religious observations even in Charlotte's correspondence, but any open rebellion on Emily's part would, like George Eliot's renunciation of her belief, surely have been recorded. We tend to forget how very reserved Emily was about her deepest thoughts, and how churchgoing and regular religious observance, thought rather eccentric in our day, were taken for granted in the time of the Brontës.

Even today religion is a serious business in a clergyman's household, and Mr Brontë was a serious clergyman in a serious age, when the authority of a father, at any rate over his daughters, was rarely challenged. Backsliding on the part of Charlotte, Emily and Anne would have been very difficult; there is little to suggest that they ever openly challenged their father's authority on any matter, and particularly little evidence for any challenge on religion. There is an occasional sign of irritation in Charlotte's letters with the odd clergyman, such as Mr Brontë's friends, Mr Morgan or Mr Jenkins, the Anglican clergymen in Brussels, and the curates who receive short shrift in *Shirley* must have been modelled on real individuals. But it was the failure of these members of the Church to live up to the standards of Christianity which irritated Charlotte both in her life and in her fiction.

Clergymen do not play a particularly prominent or glorious

part in the novels of the Brontës, but that does not mean we should dismiss them as atheistical productions, as some contemporary reviewers did. In *Jane Eyre* Mr Brocklehurst is a savage satire on extreme Evangelical clergymen, hypocritical and cruel, keeping the poor future governesses in their place while his aristocratic family enjoys luxury. Evangelicals rather oddly did very often adopt a conservative attitude in politics, and some of them were aristocratic, but it is likely that Charlotte was combining several of her pet hates in the person of Mr Brocklehurst, and it is a mistake to assume that all aspects of Mr Brocklehurst are drawn from his supposed original, the Rev. Carus Wilson.

St John Rivers is linked with Brocklehurst by the common image of the pillar, by his Evangelical views which appear perilously close to Calvinism, and by his bullying of Jane. On the other hand, St John has an attractive side to his character; his labours for the poor of his parish, his missionary zeal which leads him out to India, and even his asceticism have much to commend themselves in Jane's eyes, and she ends the novel not with the happy life of the Rochesters, but with the impending martyrdom of St John in India. The story of this heroic death owes something to the history of Henry Martyn, a famous character in the Evangelical pantheon, about whom Charlotte would have heard from her father. The rather unsatisfactory way in which St John Rivers appears initially to be a sympathetic friend, then behaves like a cold and unattractive tyrant, and ends the novel in a blaze of glory would seem to reflect Charlotte's rather mixed feelings towards the Evangelical faith of her father.

Anne Brontë's first novel also contains a bevy of clergymen. Like Jane Eyre, Agnes Grey has a father who is a poor clergyman married to a wife from a rich family, disinherited for her unwise match. This simple dichotomy between wealth and virtue is taken up later in the novel when the good Mr Weston espouses the humble Agnes, while the more frivolous Mr Hatfield pursues in vain the flirtatious Rosalie Murray. Unfortunately the crude nature of this message is such that at times we find Agnes's family and her suitor rather dull and, in spite of their troubles and their lack of religion, Rosalie Murray and Mr Hatfield appear to be characters with more potential interest.

The gap between Anne's overt intentions and the hidden meaning of her narrative is even more obvious in *Wildfell Hall*, a novel less full of clergymen than *Agnes Grey*, but more full of religion. The clergy are represented by the Rev. Michael Millward who, with his affection for malt liquors and contempt for Helen Huntingdon's mollycoddling of her son, is clearly not an Evangelical clergyman. Since we rarely see him discussing religious matters it is hard to tie him down to any religious faction in the Church. In a way he may seem to be a rare representative in the Brontë novels of the High and Dry Church, a type of clergyman probably very common in the eighteenth century before the Evangelical movement made the Church aware of its spiritual rather than its social function.

Religion appears in *Wildfell Hall* in perhaps too obvious a fashion. Before marrying Huntingdon, Helen discusses with her aunt the problem of eternal damnation. Helen says that even the wicked do not deserve to be condemned to perpetual punishment in Hell, and cites thirty passages of scripture to support her case. Disarmingly she acknowledges that she does not know Greek and, worryingly, if she had, her case would not have looked so good. We know that Anne Brontë was troubled at times by Calvinistic fears of her own damnation, but that in the later stages of her life she took the unorthodox Universalist position that even the most hardened sinner eventually is rewarded with salvation. This would seem to be Helen's attitude in her argument with her aunt, although confusingly this argument occurs during the discussion of the merits of marrying Arthur Huntingdon, in which discussion Helen is undoubtedly wrong and her aunt right.

Equally confusing is the issue of Arthur Huntingdon's salvation or damnation. Convinced of her husband's wickedness, Helen yet returns to nurse him in his final illness. Her behaviour seems odd, although she is perhaps fleeing temptation in the shape of Gilbert Markham. Once she has returned to Grassdale Manor she treats Arthur in rather a sanctimonious fashion and regrettably, but understandably, he takes to the bottle again, thus bringing on gangrene from which he dies in fear and agony. It is difficult to see why Helen is so confident of his eventual salvation, although possibly Anne had worked out a rather masochistic doctrine whereby it is Helen's suffering which eventually secures Arthur's redemption.

We see in *Wildfell Hall*, as we see in *Jane Eyre*, a certain tension between the claims of religion, a dogmatic Evangelical form of Christianity as represented by St John Rivers, Helen Burns and even Helen Huntingdon in her more self-righteous moments, and the claims of common-sense and compassion which Helen shows at times in recognising her love for Gilbert Markham and her feeling that sinners can be saved, and Jane Eyre shows in loving Mr Rochester, by normal standards an obvious candidate for damnation. In Emily Brontë's novel, religion hardly gets its fair share. The ineffective curate who abandons the fruitless attempt to educate the young Earnshaws is about the only clergyman to appear in the novel unless we count the Rev. Jabez Branderham who appears as a boring, long-winded, self-righteous and pharisaical clergyman in Lockwood's first dream. The coincidence of Jabez's initials with those of the Rev. Jacob Bunting, a prominent Methodist of the first decades of the nineteenth century, has led some to believe that here Emily is deliberately satirising a character who had gained in spite or because of his gifts of organisation both notoriety and unpopularity as the Pope of Methodism. Certainly the harshly comic way in which Branderham is attacked reminds us of the crude satires made against Non-conformist church services in the juvenilia of Charlotte and Branwell. Joseph's sour and hypocritical denunciations of anybody and everybody but himself as wicked sinners is equally mocked, although Nelly Dean's more conventional piety, not greatly interested in any nice distinctions of theological sects, does not come off much better.

But if Emily's novel seems hostile to religion it is permeated with religious imagery. Heathcliff is frequently associated with the Devil and Hell. Charlotte, when she says Heathcliff stands unredeemed in her Biographical Preface, clearly takes these references literally, as do most of the characters in *Wuthering Heights*, but Heathcliff himself, when he refers to Hell, more often means the torture to which he and Catherine are subjected when parted from each other. We are uncertain at the end of the novel whether they ever gain the heaven of reunion, and how far this heaven corresponds to the orthodox Heaven. When Lockwood gazes at the graves of Heathcliff, Edgar Linton and Catherine and says that he cannot imagine unquiet slumbers for those quiet sleepers beneath the earth, we do not know if this is conventional piety or a profound insight into the way we gain, through suffering, our reward in the next world.

Shirley is a much less exciting novel than *Wuthering Heights*, but was a work which aroused controversy in its day owing to its unflattering portrait of the clergy. Charlotte is not raising fundamental questions about the value of Christianity, merely pouring scorn on the inability of those who profess Christianity to live up to its ideals. The virtuous Mr Hall who does try to practice what he preaches emerges as something of a hero. Shirley voices unorthodox opinions, although eventually tamely marrying Louis Moore, and in her tirades we can see something of a protest, now topical, against the male dominance of the clergy. Mr Helstone has no particular qualifications for being a clergyman, although he has more refinement than the rough Mr Malone, more sincerity than the pretentious Mr Donne, and more spirit than the timid Mr Sweeting. The curates talk about theological niceties, but lack any religious feeling. Their High Church hostility to Non-conformity and thus to the workers' agitations betrays a lack of sensitivity to the plight of their fellow men. On the other side, Charlotte is not sympathetic to the cause of the revolutionaries, where extreme dissenters are accused of being insincere rabble-rousers, whose personal conduct is deplorable.

In the time she wrote *Shirley*, Charlotte lost both her sisters. Even if she had felt particularly close to Branwell, this greater loss must have affected her more, and we find less interest in the problem of eternal punishment for sinners in Charlotte's last two novels. Emily's death, sudden and strange, and Anne's death, long awaited and endured with Christian resignation, must have caused Charlotte a great deal of heart searching. She must have prayed for their recovery, and her prayers, as she sombrely acknowledges in *Shirley*, were not answered. A less brave and a less pious woman might have lost her faith. Charlotte suffered greatly, and both the latter half of *Shirley* with its rather contrived happy ending and *Villette* with its ambiguous unhappy ending reflect this suffering but, though she questions the working of Providence in both novels, she never lost her childhood faith. Towards the end of her life Mrs Gaskell reports her carrying out her duties of visiting the poor in Haworth, and when married to Mr Nicholls she performed the duties of a clergyman's wife without complaint, although one cannot help feeling that her bright spirit was dimmed in so doing.

Charlotte's last novel, *Villette*, like her first novel, *The Professor*, is set in a foreign land that is obviously Belgium and its main religious interest lies in its attacks upon Roman Catholicism. In both novels Roman Catholics are linked to Methodists as being hypocritical and exclusive, and we find the same attacks in Charlotte's juvenilia and poetry where religion, though not conspicuous, does play some part. As the daughter of a Church of England clergyman Charlotte could be expected to resent both Non-conformists and Roman Catholics, and Mr Brontë's links with both faiths appears to have led to no sympathy with them. What Charlotte resented was the way in which particular sects were quite ready to damn to eternity all who did not join them, and the way in which the mere act of joining was considered an adequate passport to salvation, irrespective of any other form of good conduct. In *Villette*, Catholics are also accused of spying and deceit. Charlotte's dislike of foreigners and her feelings for M. Heger are of course mixed up in these accusations, and we must not forget that the Catholic Paul Emanuel, and even more oddly Père Silas, are praised. On the other hand, the sinister part played by nuns, real or imaginary, in *Villette* reflects a common prejudice against the Roman Catholic Church in the nineteenth century, hard to grasp in the twentieth century, to the effect that there was something unnatural in a woman taking the vows of a nun. Eliza Reed in *Jane Eyre*, who takes up a position in an Anglo-Catholic order, is shown to be a calculating and unfeeling woman, bargaining for a place in heaven in the same way as, when a child, she struck a hard bargain for her poultry.

Charlotte's own passionate nature rejected the idea of being a nun, although the loneliness of her life after the death of her sisters had certain features in common with that of a nun. Caroline Helstone's speculations on her fate as an eternal spinster seem far fetched, and Lucy Snowe's loneliness seems almost too bad to be true, but Charlotte's own position, isolated in Haworth, and diffident about venturing in society, wracked by ill health and lack of self-confidence, seems not much better. The acceptance of the not very attractive Mr Nicholls, whose own Anglo-Catholicism and hatred of Dissenters, must have caused Charlotte anxiety, becomes understandable in the context of this loneliness.

The visit of Lucy Snowe to the confessional in *Villette* is based upon a real incident in Belgium which Charlotte reported to Emily.[4] At first sight the confessional seems to represent all that Charlotte would have found most antipathetic in Catholicism. It was a ritual which, rather than encouraging good conduct, seemed to encourage sin, since grave wrongdoing could be pardoned at the cost of a few nominal acts of penitence. Moreover, although the priest was not supposed to reveal the secrets of the confessional, it is odd how well informed Père Silas and his friends are about Lucy Snowe's doings, and no doubt Charlotte saw the confessional as a symptom of Catholic spying. And yet the confessional in particular and Catholicism in general did offer to Charlotte two comforts which she badly needed in her lonely year in Belgium and her still more lonely years after her sisters' deaths.

These two comforts were certainty and fellowship. Members of exclusive sects may be fairly unkind to those who do not belong to them, but they do look after their own. Oddly enough as daughters of the clergyman in an Anglican parish, the Brontës were isolated above the members of their father's congregation, just as they were isolated below their employers as governesses in spite of the Anglican connections of their employers. Charlotte said she thought, 'Methodism, Quakerism and the extremes of High and Low Churchism foolish, but Roman Catholicism beats them all'.[5] Elsewhere she said she loved the Church of England with all its faults.[6] Her loyalty to the Church in spite of her isolation and doubts, and Emily's doubts about all religion are not surprising. In their books we see both Emily and Charlotte using both doubt and loneliness to good effect. For all its faults the Church of England has, unlike some of its rivals, kept an interest in the world, and the Brontë novels, which could easily have retreated in arid mysticism, do keep their feet upon the ground. Questioning, arguing, quarrelling, doubting, the Brontë novels made uncomfortable reading for the clerical establishment, but this establishment was itself riven by dissent and doubt, and we can salute both Emily and Charlotte for their achievements in both reflecting and rejecting Victorian religious discomfort.

4

Schooling

Schools and education play a large part in the Brontës' lives and in their novels. Mr Brontë had risen from obscurity through being a good student and a good schoolmaster to the relative grandeur and financial security which in the nineteenth century a position as a clergyman offered. His daughters could not aspire to this, Branwell's inclinations did not lie in that direction, and neither the schools the Brontës attended, nor the private lessons which he and Miss Branwell gave to the children seemed to have fitted them very well for the world. But we must not be too harsh on Mr Brontë, trying like many parents to educate his children on limited means at a time when good schools were few and far between.

The educational reforms in England both in schools financed by the state or by the church or the misleadingly entitled public or independent schools, really belong to the second half of the nineteenth century, and education for girls always lagged well behind that of boys. Thomas Arnold was headmaster of Rugby School from 1829 to 1842, but his influence did not reach other schools until about ten years after his death. Cheltenham Ladies' College was founded in 1853 and teachers like Miss Buss and Miss Beale gradually established the right of women, in the second half of the nineteenth century, to an education on equal terms with men. Miss Beale had some harsh things to say about Cowan Bridge,[1] but it took a long time for the ideas of these pioneers to seep through to the kind of schools where the Brontës learnt and taught. Compulsory free education did not exist in England until 1870.[2]

Probably the Brontës would have suffered even worse if they had been boys. There are vague traditions of Branwell attending a decayed grammar school in Oxenhope, but it would seem that this was not a success. Even the most famous schools for boys at this time were full of brutality and ignorance, and Dickens' portraits of the establishments of Mr Squeers and Mr Creakle are not grossly exaggerated pictures of inferior schools. By contrast, even Lowood in fiction and Cowan Bridge in fact seem to have redeeming features in, for example, the presence of the kindly Miss Temple who is supposed to have an original, and other teachers who later wrote generously about Cowan Bridge. Miss Wooler's school where Charlotte both learnt and taught seems to have been a pleasant establishment, although neither Anne nor Emily was happy there as a pupil, and Charlotte suffered as a teacher.

Roe Head and Cowan Bridge were not as dissimilar as has sometimes been made out. Both had strong clerical links. We know about the Rev. Carus Wilson; two of Miss Wooler's sisters married clergymen. In addition while it is known that the purpose of Cowan Bridge was to train girls for their proper station in life, and that governess was the chief profession intended, it is worth remembering that a number of the contemporaries of Charlotte at Roe Head also became governesses. Thus, though we condemn Cowan Bridge as cruel and despise Roe Head as unenlightened, we should not forget the religious and academic quality of both schools.

It is true that the length of time the Brontës were at school was comparatively short. Maria and Elizabeth Brontë went to Cowan Bridge on 1 July 1824, and they were followed by Charlotte on 10 August and Emily on 26 November. Maria left on 14 February, Elizabeth on 31 May and Charlotte and Emily on 1 June 1825. These dates are taken from the Cowan Bridge register and suggest that Mr Brontë retained confidence in the school until after the death of Maria at home on 6 May. The registers sternly state that the intended career of Maria, but not Elizabeth, was governess, and they are fairly scathing about the intellectual attainments of all four Brontës. Charlotte who was much admired for her cleverness at Roe Head was said to read tolerably, write indifferently, work neatly, cipher a little, and know nothing of Grammar, Geography, History or Accomplishments; and Emily, who was very young when she went to Cowan Bridge, was declared to read very prettily and work a little. Ciphering presumably meant arithmetic, work may mean needlework. The reports suggest high if exacting standards, and it is also to the credit of the school that infectious diseases were recorded.[3]

After leaving Cowan Bridge the Brontës remained at home for five and a half years. The girls were educated by Miss Branwell, while Mr Brontë taught Branwell, whose time at school must have been either very short or non-existent. These years saw the inception of the juvenilia and were extremely important in the Brontës' literary development. We would like to know what Miss Branwell taught and what were her qualifications for teaching. Close cooperation between Charlotte and Branwell meant that Charlotte derived some benefit at second hand from her father's teaching; although she and her sisters learnt little Latin and Greek, they learnt about the classical world at second hand. Miss Branwell is unlikely to have been proficient in French, and Charlotte's precocious translation of *The Henriade* in 1830 almost certainly owes something to a previous translation. An early letter in French to Ellen Nussey in October 1832 is full of schoolgirl howlers. As a good Methodist Miss Branwell is likely to have been strong on the Bible. Mr Brontë talked freely with his family about politics, and entertained them with strange stories of his Irish past and the wild doings of his Yorkshire neighbours.

The greatest gift Mr Brontë and Miss Branwell gave to the young Brontës was the thirst for education and the freedom, within limited means, to find it where they could. Modern children are confined by the restrictions of examinations which limit them in a world of greater resources than the Brontës enjoyed. Modern headmasters complain, probably rightly, about the restrictions placed on their stationery and library budget, but would have found it hard to cope with the tiny scraps of paper which the Brontës used for their juvenile writing. Nor would they have found very congenial the library at Ponden House which the young Brontës certainly used at this stage.

We have the catalogue of this library and its principal feature is the antiquity of the books. It is possible that the Heaton family may have kept the modern books for their own use, not putting them up for sale, and although the Brontës were unfamiliar with contemporary novels they did know about romantic poetry. The absence of any nineteenth-century works in the catalogue may therefore be misleading. Among the books which the catalogue does show were in the library we can notice the large quantities of poetry, good, bad and indifferent, the rhyming dictionaries and the licentious works, which helped to give the juvenilia an un-Victorian flavour.

The Brontës' reading is discussed in the next chapter. We are here concerned with their writing which had, in the case of

Branwell and Charlotte, developed well before the latter went to school. In an age of easy and instant entertainment and a general reluctance to engage in literary pursuits, it seems odd to find children amusing themselves by writing, but it was not odd in Victorian times, especially when the family concerned were precocious, had literary inclinations, and were thrown upon each other's company. What was odd about the Brontës was the extent to which this writing took hold of their imagination, and the way in which they retained their interest in writing long past adolescence.

In 1826 Mr Brontë bought some wooden soldiers for Branwell and the children began imagining stories about them. Nothing survives in writing before 1829, but Charlotte claims to have established 'plays' about Young Men in June 1826, Our Fellows in July 1827, Islanders in December 1827 and bed plays in December 1827 and March 1828. We do not know what happened to Our Fellows or the bed plays, but the Young Men and the Islanders soon merged into the beginnings of the great Angrian saga, although Angria was not actually invented until 1833. Charlotte and Branwell wrote a series of stories and some other literary essays about the adventures of a group of voyagers who had travelled to West Africa. There they founded a colony known as Verreopolis or Verdopolis, sometimes as the Great Glass Town Confederacy. The children had some knowledge of African geography from reading books by Mungo Park in the Ponden House library and articles in *Blackwood's Magazine*, but the scenery of Verdopolis was unrealistically full of Regency architecture and the behaviour of the characters was derived from the same period.

A principal character in the early narratives was the Duke of Wellington who had become Prime Minister of Britain in 1828, thirteen years after his defeat of Napoleon at Waterloo. As a politician he was less successful than as a general, but remained a hero to the Brontës for all their life. Some of the early stories reflect actual political events, such as the concern over Catholic emancipation in 1829, or the love affair between the eldest son of the Duke of Wellington, the Marquess of Douro, and Marian Hume, the daughter of his father's physician. Gradually, any connections with history become severed and the Duke of Wellington was replaced by Douro as Charlotte's chief character, especially when he carved for himself the separate kingdom of Angria.

Branwell's chief hero, Alexander Percy, sometimes known as Northangerland, was the Prime Minister of this kingdom and his rivalry with Douro, also called Zamorna, became the main feature of the stories and poetry of both Charlotte and Branwell.

These stories lasted until 1839, and even after that date Charlotte wrote stories with Angrian characters in a Yorkshire setting. Critics have naturally been keen to see traces of Zamorna, who became increasingly masterful and immoral as the years passed, in the heroes of Charlotte's later novels, although these are both more realistic and well behaved. Branwell's stories, still hardly edited at all, have been dismissed as dull chronicles of war and political intrigue, far inferior to Charlotte's love stories, but neither the destruction nor the evaluation is wholly fair. Both the two elder Brontës appear to have worked closely together, and the experience probably taught Charlotte a good deal about politics, geography and history. She still had a good deal to learn about how to write, as the juvenile stories and poems are almost without exception incoherent and uncontrolled.

Emily and Anne had broken away from Charlotte and Branwell at some stage before 1834 to write their own stories about Gondal. This realm was set in the North Pacific and seemed more rugged than Angria. Many of its characters have Scottish or Irish names. With only the poetry surviving, it is difficult to conjecture even the outline of the Gondal saga. A passionate love affair between a character called Augusta and a character called Julius seems important. Death and separation, pride and unlawful love appear, as in *Wuthering Heights*, to play a major part in Gondal.

The Brontë sisters appear to have taken different attitudes to their writing. Charlotte, especially when she was on her own at Roe Head as a teacher, was worried by its dangerous attraction and by the ability of her fantastic creations to take her away from the world completely. She made more than one effort to abandon Angria, eventually saying farewell to it completely. Emily and Anne continued longer with Gondal although, judging by the evidence of the birthday notes which rather pathetically the sisters wrote every four years, Emily found Gondal more exciting than Anne did. Probably all three sisters changed their attitudes at different times, and we should not pay too much attention to Charlotte's occasional note of anxiety or Emily's joy in the rascals as she rather quaintly dubbed her characters.[4]

How far the Brontës benefited from the practice of thinking and writing about Angria and Gondal is another open question. The prose stories were written at great speed with little regard for the niceties of spelling or punctuation or coherence. Verse provided a better discipline, although even here much of both Charlotte's and Emily's early verse is rambling and fragmentary. It is probably a mistake to think of the juvenilia as a kind of apprenticeship in writing. Some of Emily's early poetry shows some promise, but it was not until Charlotte abandoned Angria for the real world, and until both sisters went to Belgium that they became proper writers.

More formal education came in lessons at home and at Miss Wooler's school. Miss Branwell seems to have been a strict disciplinarian and, considering how little time the Brontës were at school, she would appear to have achieved considerable success. Charlotte helped to teach her younger sisters when she came home in 1832. It is unlikely that Miss Branwell knew much French. Anne Brontë had a minimal knowledge of Latin, but we do not know where or when she learnt this. As one might expect, the Brontës were well grounded in scripture; Charlotte's knowledge of the Bible caused amazement among her fellow pupils at Roe Head, and the novels of all three sisters are full of scriptural references and imagery.

Charlotte went to Roe Head in January 1831 and returned in May 1832. As we can learn from her correspondence when she was a teacher, holidays were short and there were not many visits in the term to and from home. Nevertheless Charlotte does not seem to have suffered from homesickness. She did make two close friends in Ellen Nussey and Mary Taylor. The latter has left an interesting account of her oddness and precocity. She soon emerged as head of the class and carried off three prizes. Originally Miss Wooler had not thought to put Charlotte in the first class. Intellectual competition may not have been very great. Some girls became governesses like Charlotte, but others appeared to do nothing with their lives. Ellen Nussey was in the latter category, although not as prosperous as is sometimes made out, or as some of her schoolfellows. Mary Taylor's family was certainly not rich. The school, with only about ten pupils all of roughly the same age, was clearly less forbidding than Cowan Bridge which had more pupils, some of them far older than the Brontë children.

We would like to know more about the syllabus of the school. In 1835 Charlotte wrote a famous letter to Ellen Nussey urging a course of reading on her, but since Ellen had been a pupil at the same time as Charlotte, one should, unless Ellen was unusually idle or backward, be able to exclude the extensive course of English literature and some history, geography, and natural history which Charlotte recommends. Presumably these are books which Charlotte had been reading in between her time at Roe Head as a pupil and her time as a teacher. When she was a teacher we do have the odd reference, usually uncomplimentary, to odd parts of the syllabus, such as the dreaded fifth section of Repetitions (probably Scripture) and Geography problems. Rote learning must have been boring to the imaginative Brontës. It must have been doubly boring for Charlotte to have to teach what she had already learnt, although she lasted longer as a teacher than either Emily or Anne as a pupil. Oddly enough Anne was more of a success than her sisters as a governess, and Emily, whose formal education cannot have lasted more than about nine months, was reasonably successful as a teacher at Law Hill. This is perhaps a tribute to Charlotte's success in passing on her learning. Charlotte's almost imperceptible transition from pupil to teacher both at home and at Roe Head, and even in Belgium, may seem odd to us today, but was fully in accordance with current educational practice. Back in Ireland Mr Brontë had started on the long road to Haworth by being first a promising pupil and then an assistant teacher. The National Schools started by Dr Bell relied on the monitorial method whereby teachers taught a selected group of senior pupils who then passed on their knowledge to their juniors.[5] Two of Charlotte Brontë's acquaintances when she was famous, Matthew Arnold and Sir James Kay-Shuttleworth, spoke against the mechanical features of this system. Oddly enough Charlotte disliked both men, though respecting their achievements, but when at Miss Wooler's she seemed to dislike the dreary nature of her task.

Miss Wooler's was of course a private school and in many ways more enlightened than the church or state schools which were struggling to establish educational standards in the nineteenth century. We hear odd scraps of information about life at Roe Head which are surprising. Thus a very early letter from Charlotte to Ellen Nussey mentions a lecture on Galvanism, which presumably involved primitive electrical experiments.[6] Poetry was studied at Roe Head, although only in short extracts; Mary Taylor, who said that her philistine family despised poetry, declared that

Charlotte knew the long poems from which they had to study extracts. As at Cowan Bridge Charlotte was said to know little grammar and geography when she came. Grammar presumably meant old-fashioned English grammar, parts of speech and parsing which Charlotte mentions, treated as an inferior kind of Latin grammar. The Brontës were surprisingly bad at the mechanics of English until the time they wrote their novels, but the practice in grammar may have improved their French, and later Emily's German. Geography seems a surprising weakness in view of the interest in and knowledge of foreign parts displayed in the tales of Angria and Gondal. The mature novels too, whether set in Belgium or Yorkshire, show a keen sense of local geography.

Attempts have been made from the evidence of the Brontës' schoolbooks to glean a little more of the curriculum. Magnall's *Questions* and Lindley Murray's *Grammar* are supposed to have belonged to Charlotte and these, and some of the books recommended to Ellen Nussey, are part of the syllabus recommended as early as 1773 by a Mrs Chapone in a book addressed to a niece of twelve, and entitled *Letters on the Improvement of the Mind*.[7] The seriousness of this title in spite of the tender age of its original recipient makes up in part for the old-fashioned nature of the syllabus enjoined.

We do not learn much about games at Miss Wooler's, although there were occasional dramatic productions. Sewing appears to have played a large and dull part in the lives of the Brontës; attention to fine work in a poor light cannot have helped Charlotte's poor sight. It was poor sight that prevented Charlotte from advancing far in music, but Emily was good enough to teach the subject, and the poetry of both her and Anne seems very close to songs sung round the piano. Lessons in art would appear to have taken place at Roe Head. At one stage Charlotte was spending up to nine hours a day practising painting.[8] It is Anne's heroines who try to earn their living by painting, but there are plenty of actual and verbal pictures in Charlotte's novels.

There is a slightly disconnected and trivial air about this teaching, and we are reminded of the harsh verdict on girls' education by Elizabeth Barrett Browning in 'Aurora Leigh':

> I danced the polka and Cellarius,
> Spun glass, stuffed birds, and modelled flowers in wax,
> Because she liked accomplishments in girls.[9]

There are schools in nineteenth-century fiction rather like Miss Wooler's. Miss Goddard's seminary in *Emma* was perhaps a bit duller; Miss Pinkerton's academy in *Vanity Fair*, a bit more exciting. Both were a little more aristocratic than Róe Head. There is a good portrait of a school very similar to Miss Wooler's in a novel almost contemporary with *Jane Eyre*, G. H. Lewes's *Rose, Blanche and Violet*. All three establishments existed to produce young ladies, as did Miss Wooler, inculcating polite behaviour and a variety of minor accomplishments.

The genteel nature of Miss Wooler's establishment is clear. When the Brontës wanted to set up their own school, they clearly had Roe Head in mind. It is difficult to see how even a few pupils could have fitted into the parsonage, and the roughness of Haworth must have put off prospective applicants. Miss Wooler lived in a more respectable and fashionable part of Yorkshire, and with her clerical connections must have seemed a very safe character to whom to entrust one's daughter. The references in the letter recommending reading to Ellen Nussey to possible objections to Shakespeare and Byron on the grounds of coarseness suggest that Miss Wooler's was a prudish establishment. Ellen Nussey, if we can judge by her censorship of Charlotte's correspondence, was extremely prudish, whereas Charlotte clearly felt a tension between this prudery and the normal feelings of adolescence heightened by a vivid imagination and her own wide reading in pre-nineteenth-century literature. Victorian prudery which found the Brontë novels shocking did not suddenly spring up when Queen Victoria came to the throne: the Rev. Thomas Bowdler first expurgated Shakespeare in 1806.[10]

The Brontës seem to have escaped this prudish repression. Emily who was least long at Miss Wooler's escaped most easily in that her novel clearly has nothing to do with the prudish and snobbish sentiments inculcated by the average school for young ladies. Charlotte was longer at Miss Wooler's, and her attitude to what Miss Wooler was trying to do is more ambiguous. There is a certain amount of snobbery in Charlotte's works. The young ladies in *Shirley* see little and know less of the working classes with whose plight they are meant to be sympathising, just as no doubt the young ladies of Roe Head were carefully sheltered from meeting the workers in the large manufacturing towns nearby. In spite of her shocking reputation, Charlotte's heroines, if unconventional, are highly moral; nor, though she had something to say on the position of women, is she nearly as outspoken as contemporary detractors and modern admirers would have us believe. Apart from Lucy Snowe, Charlotte's heroines end up by tamely marrying, just as Charlotte herself finally married a man much inferior to herself with Miss Wooler appropriately giving the bride away.

On strictly educational matters all three Brontës do seem both to reflect and reject their schooling, although it was perhaps their experiences as teachers and in Belgium which formed their views. These will be discussed in a later chapter. Anne who was ill and unhappy at Roe Head where, however, she won a prize for good conduct, appears to speak out fairly strongly against the conventional education of young girls when she makes both Agnes Grey and Helen Huntingdon so helpless. Helen in bringing up her own son is determined that he should see life's pitfalls early on, and suggests that she would treat her daughter in the same way. This is thought very shocking. On the other hand Agnes's young pupils, and Huntingdon and his unregenerate friends clearly do not make the best use of the formal education that they enjoy. Nature and nurture both conspire to make Huntingdon bad, although on the whole Anne took the orthodox religious view that anyone could improve through their own efforts.

So, in a way, does Emily in *Wuthering Heights* albeit in a less orthodox fashion. Those who have the benefits of education in this novel are Hindley, who goes to college (something rather vaguely described) and presumably Edgar Linton, whose bookish tastes are sneered at by Catherine. Heathcliff, deliberately deprived of education by Hindley, by some mysterious means manages to turn himself into a gentleman; it is even hinted that he, like Mr Brontë, became a sizar at Cambridge, earning his keep at the University by performing menial tasks for the other students. Hareton, deliberately deprived of education by Heathcliff, manages to educate himself with the aid of Catherine. Books which keep Linton and the older Catherine apart paradoxically become the means of uniting the younger Catherine and Hareton. Linton Heathcliff for whom his father hires a tutor gets little profit from his formal education, and we feel that Emily rather despised such education.

Charlotte's first and last novels are works about teachers and schools, reflecting their author's experiences in Belgium. Curiously both William Crimsworth and Lucy Snowe seem reactionary in their attitudes to education. Crimsworth sends his son to Eton, where he himself had been unhappy, and where he knows Victor will be unhappy. Charlotte cannot have known much about Eton except for the fact that it was the school where her hero the Duke of Wellington went. It took a long time for the new spirit of Arnold to reach eccentric and aristocratic Eton, and when Charlotte wrote *The Professor*, the school was only just recovering from the savage and incompetent rule of Thomas Keates, a headmaster in contrast to whom Mr Brocklehurst seems an angel of sweetness and light. Crimsworth and Frances Henri have, at the end of the novel, their own school, as has Lucy Snowe; we do not hear much about these schools except that they seem curiously like the establishments where Charlotte's hero and two heroines had previously taught as assistant teachers.

Jane Eyre is more a novel about education; the moral education of Jane is in a sense the subject of the story. There are, however, some odd remarks about schools and pupils, over and above the discussion of Lowood and Jane's role as a governess. We begin with the strange conceptions of schools of Bessie at Gateshead as 'places where young ladies sat in the stocks, wore back-boards, and were expected to be exceedingly genteel and precise.'[11] Jane envies their accomplishments in painting, music, needlework and French. Reality at Lowood proves very different from this peculiar establishment, and this is the point which Charlotte is presumably trying to establish, although in passing she is making a shrewd comment on the fanciful way those without education picture superior educational establishments as full of quaint customs and useless achievements. There is still a popular feeling that modern universities are full of gowns and Greek.

Lowood is sternly practical, designed to turn out good governesses, and once the cruelty and inefficiency is removed Charlotte speaks without irony of its success. Under Miss Temple it became in time a truly useful and noble institution. There is further praise of education in the shape of the school in which Jane teaches at Morton, overcoming her initial snobbishness to perceive that the young villagers, though initially ignorant, have the sparks of intellect in them, and in the good English school to which Jane envisages Adèle being sent in order to correct her French defects and turn her 'into a pleasing and obliging companion: docile, good-tempered and well-principled'.[12]

This does not seem very exciting. When Charlotte wrote *Jane Eyre* her hopes of founding a school of her own had just foundered. The two years in Belgium had filled her with affection for things English. Schools on the pattern of Miss Wooler's which seem to appear in the reformed Lowood or the school which corrected Adèle's foreign ways appear oddly attractive, in spite of the fact that Lowood is limited and Adèle, though docile, never seems likely to be interesting. By the time she finished *Shirley*, Charlotte's personal tragedies clearly dominated her life, but she had, both before and after these, been a little more exposed to horizons outside Miss Wooler's and begun to challenge attitudes, particularly attitudes to women, which she had once found acceptable. Some of the harshest comments on *Jane Eyre* and the other Brontë novels came from those who found it a shocking tale of feminine independence. Significantly Miss Wooler was one of the disapproving voices.

In *Shirley* Charlotte was anxious to speak against her detractors. Her publishers had difficulty in persuading her not to include a reply to one of the most savage of these reviews, that by Lady Eastlake, who had said that if *Jane Eyre* was written by a woman it was written by 'one who has, for some sufficient reason, long forfeited the society of her own sex'. This review was written in 1848 well after Charlotte had begun her novel with its two heroines, one of whom, Caroline Helstone, received a conventional education which she feels unduly restricts her, while the other, Shirley, is imaginatively taught by Louis Moore and holds original and independent ideas. Shirley's independence is, of course, helped by her private income and though she shows spirit in refusing the advances of the aristocratic Sir Philip Nunnely, who has intellectual pretensions of a feeble kind, her eventual surrender to marriage with Louis Moore seems a little tame in a book which at times appears to be uttering a strangled plea for proper education. Caroline also ends up by conventionally marrying Robert Moore, but not before she has been the subject of some fairly savage attacks on the kind of education for which women were being prepared. Thus Mr Helstone says 'stick to the needle – learn shirt-making and gown-making, and pie-crust making, and you'll be a clever woman some day'.[13]

Lucy Snowe in *Villette* has no private means and yet fights her way to some kind of fulfilment through her intellect, just as Charlotte Brontë had fought her way to some kind of recognition as an author by the time she came to write *Villette*. Since the only success in their lives came with the writing of their books, they must have felt grateful to the education which enabled them to achieve these triumphs, even though their formal education seems so scanty and old fashioned, and even though initially it fitted them not for the profession of author, but of teacher.

5

Reading

On the face of things, the Brontës' education was remarkably slight and provincial. This provincial tone does in some measure appear in their published works, but it will not do to take at its face value Charlotte's view, exemplified in her Preface to *Wuthering Heights*, that Emily's work is 'rustic all through'. From small children the whole family were avid readers totally chewing up what they read and discussing it among themselves before their own work issued in print, at first the mock print of their small magazines and juvenile tales, then the real print of poems and novels.

Their first and most intimately known book was surely the Bible. As an Evangelical family, they were brought up on its pages so that when, in *Wildfell Hall*, Helen comes to search the New Testament for texts dealing with Hell and forgiveness, her creator is able to quote chapter and verse without difficulty. All the girls stitched samplers in which they copied biblical passages. Emily, who refused to teach in Sunday school, could easily have shown herself mistress of the whole book. This stands her in good stead when she wishes to satirise the Calvinistic Methodists in *Wuthering Heights*.[1] When Mr Brontë put a mask on each of his children and asked them questions, Charlotte had no hesitation in answering that the Bible was the best book in the world, and there are echoes of it in all her novels.

Sunday by Sunday the little Brontës read Bible, prayer-book and hymns. Often the hymns seem to have been printed out on special sheets, of which many still survive in the parsonage at Haworth. The rhythms of the hymns pervade many of the sisters' adult poems. Anne wrote her own hymns, some of which are still sung, and the better known sisters, Emily and Charlotte, constantly used hymn metres and vocabulary. The eighteenth-century imagery of Newton is echoed in:

> There let thy bleeding branch atone
> For every torturing tear:
> Shall my young sins, my sins alone
> Be everlasting here?

And in her reply to William Weightman's valentine of 1840, Charlotte tells the young curate:

> Where'er you go, however far
>   In future years you stray,
> There shall not want our earnest prayer
>   To speed you on your way.
>
> A stranger and a pilgrim here
>   We know you sojourn now;
> But brighter hopes, with brighter wreaths,
>   Are doomed to bind your brow.[2]

It is a parody of eighteenth-century hymnology, a mock heroic of Evangelicalism. The hymn vocabulary and hymn rhythms entered the deepest memory of the Brontë sisters and return unconsciously in the rhythms of *Jane Eyre* and *Wuthering Heights*.

As soon as they could read, the Brontë children devoured the newspapers. There is an authenticated story of the eldest, Maria, retiring to the little room above the hall and returning with the political and national news in her grasp. The others followed suit. It was paternal example that had made them such enthusiastic readers of news. Mr Brontë had engaged in several controversies in the *Leeds Intelligencer* and *Leeds Mercury* before they were born, and he continued to read the papers regularly.

The literary magazines were also available, especially *Blackwood's*, and after 1831, apparently, *Fraser's*. It seems that old copies of *Blackwood's* remained in the parsonage, for the children evidently read very early of the explorers Parry and Ross, Denham and Clapperton. They were filled with an enthusiasm for exploration, particularly in Africa, which they chose as the site for their imaginary lands, though Emily seems to have exerted quite early a pull to bring their fairy-tale heroes and heroines back to an English, even Yorkshire landscape.

As such, children's literature was in its infancy. The *Arabian Nights*, Aesop's *Fables* and *Gulliver's Travels* had all been intended for adults, but were eagerly seized on by these imaginative children. Their influence is not escaped even in *Jane Eyre* and *Wuthering Heights*. Emily at any rate retained her enthusiasm for the miraculous all her life, though quite early on she had tempered this with the inclination to make the marvellous seem realistic. In their early days, however, all four surviving children saw themselves as genii, controlling the lives of their tiny puppets; their model was the *Arabian Nights*. These tales laid down a foundation for the Romantic taste in the esoteric: Africa, Asia, the West Indies were all of interest.

Blackwood's included poetry, story, reviews, current affairs, polemic and many other kinds of writing. From this miscellany the children clearly took their view that literature was committed, not mere entertainment and frivolity. Works of imagination were vehicles to convey a moral purpose; even Mr Brontë had conceded that with *The Maid of Killarney*, which he wrote in 1818. In imitation of *Blackwood's* they all contributed to a series of tiny magazines of their own, many of which are still preserved at Haworth and elsewhere. Writing, in the tiny print style which all four adopted, became second nature.

The possibility of using fiction for moral purposes was deeply underlined by the popularity of Bunyan's *Pilgrim's Progress*, which Mr Brontë had known in his Irish days. Though Branwell and Emily left the 'narrow way' of pilgrimage, they remained conscious of the metaphor, while Charlotte and Anne incorporated it in prose and verse. This Evangelical classic proved most influential for its exploration of motive and the meaning behind action. Jane Eyre's perpetual self-examination, the resulting address to the reader, the deep psychological probing that this leads to, are based firmly on this seventeenth-century allegory.

The Brontë children very early began to read the stories of Sir Walter Scott. His *Tales of a Grandfather* was in the house during their teenage years, and the Scots element in Gondal is probably attributable in part to him, though a fondness for Robert Burns may have played a part in Mr Brontë's enthusiasm for Scots scenery. More obviously than the prose fiction, Scott's ballads and lyrics affected the poetry of all the Brontës. The Romantic view of landscape, or ruins by moonlight, of crags and glens and moorland in the Brontë works, is founded on Scott. Emily will use words such as 'mountain' and 'glen' to describe Haworth scenery. Her feeling for the moors round her home undoubtedly partakes of the 'open air adventure' ambience of Scott. Scott was also responsible for a regional flavour entering the novel: this was much accentuated by the Brontës, especially in *Wuthering Heights*.

Heathcliff himself may owe something to Scott. Parallels between him and the hero of *The Black Dwarf* have been drawn; but there are so many putative origins for Heathcliff that it is impossible to be sure just what influences helped Emily's interest in him. The Gondal poems sometimes take place in open, airy situations: the scenery in 'The Death of "A.G.A." ', for example, may derive in part from Scott. Charlotte shows less interest in high moorland; possibly some of the background to *Jane Eyre* may reflect Scott, but there are closer influences, including her own knowledge of Yorkshire and North Derbyshire.

Early in their lives the Brontës discovered Cowper, some of whose *Olney Hymns* were in use for congregational worship. The domesticity of 'The Task' may be reflected in the homely interiors of the novels. It seems likely that the Brontës would warm to Cowper's accounts of pet hares, and in adult life Anne studied his biography and wrote a poem addressed to him. They all found themselves moved by Cowper's word picture of 'The Castaway'; Branwell saw himself in that role, as a man tragically incapable of responding to the messages of religion, and so overwhelmed in 'darker seas' than the mere literal ocean. The notion of a man permanently cast out from God's light took hold of Emily, who uses the figure often in her poems before modifying him to make a constituent of Heathcliff. Of the other eighteenth-century poets, Edward Young was certainly known to Charlotte, and the interest in weather and climate, with their effect on the landscape, may well derive from Thomson.

There is undoubtedly an archaic flavour about the adult poems of the Brontës: they compare interestingly with those of Mrs Hemans, for example. By contrast, the Brontës' work is uncluttered, direct, inclined to reject simile and strained metaphor. This directness seems to stem from the late eighteenth-century writers, with a considerable admixture of the Romantics, especially Wordsworth and Coleridge, though it has long been thought that Byron contributed strongly to their thought. Mention also needs to be made of the Irishman Tom Moore, one of Byron's circle, who took the fancy of the Brontës in adolescence. His poems, like those of the hymn writers, were written to be sung, and the close relationship between words and melody is a feature of Brontë poetry. Several poems by Anne and Emily are entitled 'Song', a title which may be taken literally; it is hardly surprising that musical adaptations of Brontë poetry can sound natural and effective.

Several of Wordsworth's keynotes appear in Brontë poetry and prose. Perhaps the most prominent are the emphasis on the

spiritual benefits of Nature, and the idyllic experience of childhood. It is difficult to determine quite what they had read. The
lyrical ballads seem to be echoed several times in the poetry of
Emily and Anne. Emily's tendency to pantheism appears to have
been fed to some extent on Wordsworth's work, though resemblances to Shelley may be more apparent. We may also remind
ourselves of Charlotte's reply to her father, when she told him,
from under a mask placed on her as a child, that after the Bible,
the best book was 'the book of nature'.[3]

Wordsworth's emphasis on childhood is a very sympathetic
doctrine to both Charlotte and Emily. Children are well depicted
in *Villette*, but of course the prime example of Rousseauesque
belief in the innocence and spiritual insight of the child comes in
Jane Eyre, where we are shown the young Jane confounding the
dark pillar of Mr Brocklehurst with innocent directness. It may
not always be so clear that the core of *Wuthering Heights* is also a
vivid and intense childhood experience, recollected, without much
tranquillity, for the rest of Catherine's life. Of course, this return
to a blighted childhood owes much to Emily's feeling that her
own was in some way blighted, but the poetic reinforcement of
this feeling is attributable to Wordsworth. There are several poems
in which bright, spiritually aware children are drained by later
experience, as the shades of the prison-house (a favourite metaphor with Emily) close upon them. Several good poems by Anne
treat the same theme, but in *Agnes Grey*, we are shown some very
unromantic 'bad-natured' children, who do not appear to trail any
'clouds of glory'.[4]

Coleridge seems to play a larger part in Emily's poetic development than Charlotte's. The metaphor of life as a voyage, implicit
in some hymnology and Cowper, was encountered again in 'The
Ancient Mariner'. This is echoed in some of Emily's poems and is
perhaps present in the background of *Villette*, as well as *Jane Eyre*
and *Wuthering Heights*. Emily seems to have read 'Kubla Khan'
(though we have no external evidence of this), and to have been
very much attracted to 'Christabel'. Perhaps the best evidence of
this is her adoption of the rare name 'Geraldine' for her obnoxious,
cruel, passionate Gondal princess. The Irish reference in the name
may well have been an influence with her, but Coleridge seems
the most obvious source.

It was not only Geraldine's name that attracted Emily. She was
clearly much interested in the relationship between Geraldine and

Christabel. As she often seems to have seen herself as the 'bad' twin in relation to Anne's goodness, she may well have felt Geraldine haunting her. Certainly during the years after 1837 she became obsessed with the powerful, ruthless Gondal princess, Geraldine. Emily herself had quite ruthless moods at times; in these moods she could not respond to anyone's love. The personality of Coleridge's Geraldine, and her supernatural character, were sometimes appended to Emily's own.

Geraldine's presence in *Wuthering Heights* is in transmuted form. The many references to Heathcliff's strange appearance and physical characteristics do not amount to making him non-human. But there is no doubt that some of his actions and values do carry a supernatural aura. He has 'basilisk' eyes, like Geraldine's, for example. Wuthering Heights is compared to a castle similar to the setting of 'Christabel'. The Gothic aspects of the house and its inhabitants may be frequently normalised, but readers have constantly been aware of a supernatural layer to the story, which may derive some of its force from Coleridge's poem.

Charlotte Brontë makes a number of references to Shelley. It seems likely that the children had encountered him during the early 1830s, at first perhaps in Moore's *Life of Byron*, though the poems were readily available in cheap editions and they could easily have obtained copies. Emily's poetry seems often indebted to him, and there is some evidence that she may have made him a personal cult. Both she and Anne appear to have read 'Epipsychidion' at an early stage. To judge the effect that might have on an impressionable adolescent who happens, like its heroine, to be called Emily, one should re-read the poem with teenage girlhood in mind. Shelley's life and death were Romantic, the latter almost self-willed. Heathcliff's death was also self-willed, and Emily's own may have been partly so. As she grew up, Emily took a great interest in geometry and astronomy; this may also have been under Shelley's influence.[5]

It seems likely that the Brontës as children thought of Byron as the centre of the Romantic circle, around whom Shelley, Moore and Keats revolved. It has been a commonplace of Brontë criticism for many years to ascribe both Rochester and Heathcliff to the influence of the Byronic hero. Charlotte gives early evidence in the juvenilia of reading 'Childe Harold', 'Manfred' and 'Cain'. It may seem surprising that Mr Brontë did not censor the reading of children who quickly became conversant with the adulterous loves of Byron's adventurers. Apparently he did not do so, though in the letter to her friend Ellen Nussey, to which we shall soon refer, Charlotte shows that she realises the moral problem raised by the enjoyment of these poems.

As in the case of Shelley, Byron's life was as interesting as his poetry. In Moore's biographical work the Brontë children could follow his career. Incidents in his own life as well as those of his heroes are supposed to have influenced the character of Heathcliff, while the rugged ugliness and remoteness of Rochester, as well as his wandering life, inescapably suggest Byronic influence. Some of the poetry of both Charlotte and Emily seems like an appendix to Byron: there are prisoners, empty halls, voyages, hatred, black-haired wanderers and violent loves. At times this Byronic influence leads to ridiculous bathos, especially in Emily's earlier verse. Even in the mature novels, the wild emotions of Heathcliff and Rochester edge towards the absurd at times, and an early enthusiasm for Byron may be responsible.

The minor Romantic Moore may have appealed disproportionately to the young Brontës because he was Irish. Emily and Anne named a spot on the 'common' behind the parsonage, 'The Meeting of the Waters', in reference to one of his lyrics, and Anne collected his work both in printed copies and in her manuscript music book. She adopts metres which Moore had taken over from Irish tradition, and there seem to be similar, slighter echoes in Emily's poems. As adolescents, the Brontës all read Southey, to whom Charlotte later wrote in a bid to gain advice.

One well known document provided Brontë scholars with the beginning of their quest for formative influences. This is the letter Charlotte wrote to her friend Ellen Nussey at the age of eighteen giving her advice on what to read, like some sixth-form tutor advising a scholarship candidate. She recommended Shakespeare (but not the comedies) and Byron without 'Don Juan'. In particular, she mentions *Macbeth*, *Hamlet*, *Henry VIII* and *Richard III*, as valuable plays. These had been read by the young Brontës but not of course seen; in later years Charlotte was very dubious about the morality of the theatre, though all the children acted their own plays as readily as they wrote tiny magazines.[6] Among the Romantics, Charlotte advises Ellen to read Scott whose 'sweet, wild, romantic poetry can do you no harm', Wordsworth, Campbell and Southey. Scott's novels are the *only* fiction she recommends: ('all novels after his are worthless').

The tone of this letter shows that Charlotte regards education by reading as vital. This may seem unusual to an age when reading is beginning to be thought of as a hobby or fad rather than the staple of education. To Charlotte it was undoubtedly the latter, and we know from William Wright's account that Patrick had shown a similar understanding in his youth. In those remote days in County Down he had certainly read Burns as well as *Pilgrim's Progress* and 'Paradise Lost'. The themes of the latter were well represented in the paintings of John Martin, of which the young Brontës saw engravings hanging on the parsonage walls. Like Shakespeare, Milton was recommended by Charlotte to her friend and fellow student.

The library at Ponden Hall must have been like a small heaven to such mentally adventurous children as the little Brontës turned out to be. The main internal evidence for their use of the library occurs in the poems of Branwell and the varied early writings of Charlotte. It seems probable that Robert Heaton may have first offered to lend books to Mr Brontë and his children, just as in Ireland Patrick is thought to have borrowed quite freely from the library of Thomas Tighe at Parson's Hill near Drumballyroney. Only later, one supposes, would the girls and Branwell make Ponden a place of pilgrimage.[7]

Winifred Gerin was the first to point out that Branwell must have used Chateaubriand's *Travels* as the basis of one early manuscript, and there seems to be a strong link between various books of African travel, including Mungo Park's *Travels*, and the Brontës' enthusiasm for Africa, which led them to situate their imaginary lands there in the first place. These seem to have been unavailable to them except from Ponden Hall. There are many other points in the juvenilia where we must suspect an influence from the library there.

Once we accept that the Brontës used Robert Heaton's library freely, we may be amazed at the scope and nature of the books they could borrow. Most of the books had apparently been bought by Heaton's grandfather, also named Robert, who had died in 1794. A great deal of them were seventeenth- and eighteenth-century books of all possible kinds: plays, poems, records of trials, dictionaries, handbooks, natural history.

There is no doubt that the Brontës read widely in these books, discussing them, reading aloud to each other, imitating style and content. Having access to Ponden, they would feel themselves heirs to a world of knowledge and wisdom, though it must sometimes have clashed painfully with the church wisdom of Evangelicalism. They quickly set about making their own contribution to the world: they cherished, as Charlotte later said, the hope and ambition of one day becoming authors in print.

This emphasis on books is a commonplace of the time. But over and over again in *Jane Eyre*, *Villette* and *Wuthering Heights*, the book is seen as a main tool of the educating, civilising process, despite Catherine's anguished cry at finding Edgar reading in the library during her own critical illness. This attitude comes quite naturally to the Brontës: it must have been greatly strengthened by their immersion in the treasures at Ponden Hall. Though at times Emily seems to rebel against her subservience to the written word, she cannot rid herself of the world in which she finds herself happy. Charlotte's reference in *Shirley* to the heroine's 'tenacity' of her book surely reflects Emily's own character.

Their early attempts to fulfil these ambitions were not encouraging. Charlotte wrote to Robert Southey at the end of 1836 (the same month in which Emily and Anne were beginning to preserve their poems), and received a gloomy reply some months later. The poet agreed that she had 'the faculty of verse', but he tried hard to dissuade her from hoping for any kudos from it: 'Write poetry for its own sake; not in a spirit of emulation, and not with a view to celebrity'. He also pointed out sternly that as a woman she might unfit herself for her proper duties if she continued to seek distinction. Though part of the tone of the letter is clearly attributable to Southey's own experiences and disillusion, Charlotte thanked him kindly and put her ambition back into store for eight or nine years.

Branwell also had ambitions to be a writer and, in terms of convention, more need. He would have to earn his living for himself and keep a family. Portrait painting came to nothing, and he made several efforts to gain paid employment as poet and journalist. He implored the editor of *Blackwood's* rather rudely to take him on as a successor to James Hogg. His shrill demands met with no reply. He had overvalued his talent, but we should not undervalue it. Branwell obtained a reputation in Haworth and the West Riding for witty chat and humour. His satire may seem heavy handed, yet he might have reached a popular audience if he had approached the task with less bombast and pretension. When *Blackwood's* failed him, he wrote successively to Wordsworth and Hartley Coleridge.

It may have been due to the reputation of the lake poets that Branwell sought a post in early 1840 at Broughton-in-Furness, as a tutor in the family of Robert Postlethwaite. In particular, Branwell had begun to be influenced by de Quincey, not only in poetic matters, but also in the habit of taking opium. While at Broughton, he visited Hartley Coleridge, to whom he showed his translation of Horace's *Odes*. Hartley Coleridge was encouraging, urging Branwell to complete the work and promising to look at it when it was complete. This advice apparently went to Branwell's head, since he now believed he could make his way in the literary world. As a result he became careless with his tutorial duties and was soon discharged. He returned to Haworth not a bit ashamed. Such was the unreliable brother who provided for the Brontë sisters their nearest example of the species 'young man'.

Though he had long been interested in literature, Mr Brontë himself was, of course, quite unable to afford a collection of books of the scale which we have been contemplating. Though he did buy some volumes, and had kept some from his childhood, his young family would soon outgrow his small library. But he was a member of Keighley Mechanics' Institute Library and there are records of the young people attending lectures there. It is fairly certain that they borrowed books from the library.

The Mechanics' Library owned a wide variety of books, which have been listed (in a catalogue from 1841) by Mr Clifford Whone.[8] Many were volumes of philosophy and eighteenth-century science, including Astronomy and Logic. It seems likely that Emily's interest in astronomy was generated by these. There were many biographies, including the lives of Nelson, Oliver Cromwell, Scott and Sir Humphrey Davy, all of whom seem to have been interest to the Brontës. A two-volume edition of Moore's *Life of Byron* may have been used, if it cannot be proved that Mr Brontë himself possessed a copy. By 1841 the Brontës may have been less interested in travel books, but more than 150 such books were in the library, including volumes on Egypt, Spain, America, Turkey and New Zealand. The Brontës always showed interest in the world beyond England and these volumes may have helped to fuel their interest. However, books of European travel are not prominent among the collection, and we should remember the personal experiences of Belgium when accounting for Charlotte's fascination with French language and literature.

There were plenty of books on Natural History to build upon

the girls' childhood reading of Bewick. These included treatises on Geology, Botany and Zoology, as well as White's *Natural History of Selborne* and two volumes on birds. While all these provided a background to the Brontës' understanding of the world, it is impossible to tell which of them they read; there seems no trace of issue registers and internal evidence is slight. All one can legitimately say is that in the Brontë novels an awareness of the breadth of possible knowledge is shown, and that the Mechanics' Library is one of the sources of this awareness. At a much later stage, once she had met her publishers, in 1848, Charlotte was frequently sent parcels of books by the directors of Smith, Elder. These came much too late to affect Emily or Anne, but a knowledge of contemporary novel writing does seem to have some input in *Shirley* and *Villette*.

We should not neglect, in examining the writing of three women authors who created strong male characters in their books, the possible influence of their one brother, Branwell. Early commentators saw him as a major factor; he had inspired their work, perhaps even written it himself. Charlotte perhaps gave some credence to this view in explaining her sisters' work after their death, particularly in trying to account for the 'coarse' elements in *Wildfell Hall* and by hints in the Preface to the second edition of *Wuthering Heights*.

The old charge that Branwell wrote or ghosted parts of *Wuthering Heights* has by now been laid to rest. At one time, he began a novel himself, generally known as 'And the Weary are at Rest'. There are some similarities of character between it and Emily's book, but there is nothing whatever to link it to her novel. Branwell's capacity to sustain writing effort waned considerably after 1846, though as a child he had been a relentless scribbler. Emily's novel grew from her earlier writing, and there is no need to invoke Branwell to explain the forceful nature of the writing; in fact had he written it it might have been a lot less forceful.

Nor was Branwell a model for Heathcliff, Rochester, or Arthur Huntingdon. Heathcliff's mad rages and violent passions were not totally alien to Branwell: he could rave and shout finely. His crazed affection for Mrs Robinson from 1843 to 1846 certainly partook of a vehemence and obsessional quality which compares with Heathcliff. But Branwell was a puny fighter, despite his wish to enter the boxing ring, and would never have had the determination of Heathcliff to usurp the Earnshaw property. Some male characteristics may have been contributed by Branwell to the male characters in *Wuthering Heights*, but as much perhaps to Edgar as to Heathcliff. Anne's Arthur Huntingdon is very much unlike Branwell. He appears a cold suitor and colder husband; Branwell was warm-hearted and generous as well as easily wounded. There is very little in Rochester which could plausibly have been copied from Branwell.

What Branwell did do for the girls in their years of growing up was to provide both a companion and a yardstick. In some ways, he resembles the athletic pacemaker, who runs the race for all he is worth until it becomes serious; but he has never intended to win, and is unfit to do so. Branwell poured forth articles and poems, stories and political comment in the little magazines the children all wrote. In these games he was the leader. But as real poetic composition or novel writing approached, he dropped behind, turning aside in the first place to pursue visual art, and he might have become a serviceable portrait painter, if his waywardness and willingness to be sidetracked had not intervened. Branwell showed the Brontë girls that not all men had better abilities than women; even though their father's intellect had to be respected, Charlotte's younger brother could be outshone. He provided a friendly rival, held in great affection during adolescence, for Charlotte to emulate and overcome. Her observation was sharper, her understanding deeper, and her capacity for sustained work greater.

All the same, the Brontë novels and poems would not be the same without Branwell, and his part in the story should not be omitted. He could at times write good poetry in his own right; some sonnets will bear re-reading, and he could produce affecting narrative. Through him too, the girls learnt not to hold the male in awe, but to recognise that men were fallible and (as Anne emphasises in *Wildfell Hall*), as likely, or more so, to be led off the 'narrow way' as girls.

In recent years it has been realised that some of the qualities of the Brontë novels and verse are due to their persistent practice in the visual arts. Branwell was not the only member of the family to draw and paint. William Robinson, a Leeds artist, had been engaged to give lessons to him and Charlotte, and he probably gave lessons to the others too. As far back as 1829, the Brontës are found copying pictures of the Lake District from a book of illustrations brought back after a visit to the Lakes by their Uncle

Fennell. At the same time, Charlotte and Branwell were drawing small pictures in pen and ink to present to Anne.

Emily's copies of Bewick engravings are well known; it was a book of Bewick that Jane Eyre was looking at on the rainy afternoon when she was taunted by her Reid cousins. Emily chose moorland birds to copy, and at Haworth there are still some more narrative scenes from Bewick, copied in her early adolescence. Her drawing of a hawk is generally known as 'Hero' after the tame hawk she kept on the premises, but there is no certainty that Hero looked anything like this Bewick copy. What is certain is that this habit of observation was transferred to the written word. Emily's delight in moorland birds at the age of eleven shows that already she is stirred by the wild elements in Nature, and points the way to Catherine's deserted nest of lapwings.

Both Anne and Charlotte copied little country scenes, emphasising flowers and trees. The Brontës possessed books of pictures of trees, and soon became familiar with the different species. Hence the chestnut tree riven by the storm, the gaunt thorn at the Heights. The quiet January scene overlooking Thornfield in Chapter 12 of *Jane Eyre*, with its closely observed detail, bears witness to this interest in rural landscape: hawthorn and hazel bushes line the country lane, but 'there was not a holly ... to rustle.' Thus Charlotte lists the three most common hedgerow bushes, which she had observed herself in lanes around Haworth and Roe Head, alerted to the types of trees by the landscapes she had copied.

The children also drew fantastic scenes from other parts of the world or from no real world at all. They seem to have enjoyed particularly the supernatural world of John Martin, already mentioned, whom they had encountered in magazine engravings. He depicted Heaven and Hell, providing on the way an idea of how the great glass city might appear, far away in West Africa. From the Finden illustrations to Moore's *Life of Byron* the Brontës also derived great enjoyment, copying both portraits, whom they renamed as Gondal or Angrian characters, and exotic scenes of distant temples, mosques and ruins. They were also attracted to engravings of English architecture, for example, pictures of Bolton Abbey which the family visited in 1833 with Ellen Nussey. Charlotte was very short-sighted. She enjoyed country walks, over the moors and elsewhere; but she interpreted the scene through what she had drawn with her pencil in imitation of the engravers.

Drawings and paintings 'from life' (as Emily wrote of her sketch of Keeper) are rather rare in Brontë collections. It may seem strange that the children should interpose a layer of interpretation between themselves and the real world in this way. But there is no doubt that such copying trained their eyes efficiently. There would simply not have been time to stay long enough on the moors or down the Oakworth lanes to enable them to practise such detailed observation. But as Charlotte's description shows, their trained eyes could visualise the reality, when it was not there before them, all the better.

Music was an important part of the life of the Brontë children. Emily began to play the piano at the age of about ten and, from then on, each year shows additions to their music collection. Anne followed her sister, and Branwell played the flute. The surviving Brontë music is a wide-ranging mixture. There are standard piano works by Mozart, Beethoven and the early Romantics; there are popular songs, including American ballads; there are arrangements of orchestral works, and extracts from oratorio.[9] They evidently collected Handel's *Messiah* over a number of years. It is not clear what standard they all reached, but Emily was regarded highly by M. Heger in Belgium and would have started lessons with a very capable professor of music if she had returned, like Charlotte, for a second year.

Anne's surviving music copy-book, bought at Thorp Green in 1843, includes, in addition to many hymns and Irish melodies by Moore (as well as some of his Sacred Songs), items such as 'The bird let loose' by Beethoven, two or three pieces by Burns set to music, 'Come beneath the linden tree' by J. M. Wade, with music adapted from Mozart, and various other sacred material. Though this collection may have been made partly to teach the Robinson children, it is not untypical of the longer pieces to be found in the Brontë music collection subsequently owned by Ellen Nussey, and preserved at the parsonage. The novels contain many references to music as a drawing room accomplishment, but to the Brontë family it was more important than that. Their sharp ears – especially those of Emily and Anne – were nurtured on harmony, and musical cadences pervade their writings.

Though the Brontës' formal education was partial and disjointed, they came from a household where all kinds of artistic endeavour were paramount. They sought out and revelled in all kinds of artistic experience. Visual, auditory and literary arts surrounded them, and they tried their hands at everything. This attitude heightened their perceptions of all spheres, and they readily internalised their perceptions. They explored human feelings deeply, and discussed their explorations in a way that would not have been possible for one young person in isolation. They understood that rational artistic technique was important to convey these feelings. Both poems and novels show their passion for strong and ordered expression, and bear witness to the long process of artistic attunement through which they had all passed.

6

Teaching

It may seem remarkable that education runs like a thread through the themes of all the Brontë novels. At times, their discussion of matters educational becomes general, but usually it is the education of girls that is a major topic for Charlotte, and a matter of interest to both the other sisters. Pupils are a constant feature of the books, whether in groups or singly. In particular, great interest is shown in the status and work, treatment and rewards of a girls' school teacher or private governess.

All three Brontë sisters taught, and were in general horrified by the process and the apparent stupidity and uncooperative nature of their pupils. Charlotte taught for a considerable time, from 1835 until 1843, but never felt happy: 'teach ... teach ... teach ...' she says of her Dewsbury Moor experience.[1] Emily avoided this kind of work more successfully, apparently because she physically sickened when confronted with schools. But even she did not escape a period at Law Hill, Halifax, and six months in Belgium. Anne had two governess posts, at Blake Hall, Mirfield, and at Thorp Green near York. Their several experiences were pooled among the three, and aspects of all enter the works of all three.

Clear and undisputed facts about Emily's short teaching career at Law Hill are hard to come by. There are a number of almost certainly valid inferences and one or two deductions which seem very probable. The Law Hill period was undoubtedly most influential in Emily's life and contributed widely to *Wuthering Heights*. It was at Law Hill that she wrote the earliest three poems published just after her death by Charlotte and her experiences at Law Hill seem to have changed her approach to poetic expression. For all these reasons, every scrap of evidence about Law Hill is most welcome.

Law Hill is the name of a house, at one time also known as Mount Pleasant, about two miles from Halifax on the high ridge which overlooks the town on the east. Nowadays the train from Halifax to Bradford tunnels under the hill, passing beneath the

Beacon, to emerge at the foot of a gentle slope covered with green lawns, the lower end of the grounds of Shibden Hall. Law Hill cannot be seen from this end of the tunnel; it is high above and concealed by some foothills. Across a yard from the three-storey house itself is a block of buildings, still standing, which was once a woollen warehouse, then the schoolroom in which Emily worked, then a neglected building, partly turned into cottages.[2]

It is not at all clear how Emily came to hear of the post offered in this school, late in 1838, by the proprietor, Miss Elizabeth Patchett. Halifax was not a remote town for the Brontës, though to judge by the tone of some of Emily's poetry, one might think so. Branwell had friends there, and it is possible that he may have been employed at a school in the town at about the same time, though we should accept this tradition with caution. The Patchetts also had connexions in the Roe Head area; possibly the post might have been suggested through Miss Wooler. But this is all speculation. What we do know is that, by early October 1838, Emily was working at Law Hill and not particularly happy with her position.

This was the first and only time that Emily was away from home without any other relation at hand. She had been at Cowan Bridge as a child, at Roe Head briefly in 1835, and was to go to Belgium in 1842. On each occasion, at least one other sister was present. During these six months, if the 'exile' lasted so long, Emily had no member of her family to talk to. It seems almost certain that she was forced to make contact with others, among them some of the children and the proprietor. There may have been two other sub-teachers, but we do not know whether Emily shared her thoughts with them. In a poem of 7 December 1838, 'How still, how happy!' she addresses a companion on the moors, but this may be pure imagination.

The case for Emily's use of features from Halifax in *Wuthering Heights* has been made in detail elsewhere and, here, I shall treat the evidence as sufficient to describe this use as fact. Law Hill itself was regarded as a possible origin of Wuthering Heights by a number of writers in the early twentieth century, but the building is not comparable with the old farm of the Earnshaws. But Law Hill did have barns and byres attached. There were a number of farm servants, and the constant presence of dogs and other animals would be a feature previously not experienced by Emily. The aura of animal life in *Wuthering Heights* was absorbed here, in the yard where children played, between the house and schoolrooms, with the stables and cow-byres to the rear.[3]

Emily taught the younger girls, one of whom survived to tell her reminiscences of Emily to Mrs Chadwick, researching in the 1880s. Emily's own account is in 'A little while, a little while', of 4 December 1838. We may reasonably assume, despite earlier doubts, that this was written in the schoolroom or Emily's bedroom, during the evening period when the children were not in her charge. She says in the poem that this period was an hour long, though Charlotte's earlier letter mentions half an hour. Here for the first time Emily discusses her two interrelated but separate sources of poetic release. Shall she return, in imagination, to Haworth, for:

> ... what on earth is half so dear,
> So longed for as the hearth of home?

Or shall she seek 'Another clime, another sky' – Gondal? The latter, she decides; but as she describes it, Gondal sounds very like Haworth, and the 'little and a lone green lane' of Gondal is often taken for the one winding along to the moors from the far churchyard gate. Only the deer browsing seem to distinguish the imagined from the real scene.

The rest hour ends, and Emily is given back 'to weary care'. She did not, then, enjoy teaching at all. Her lonely communing with poetry pleased her much more. But it does seem quite likely that she gained a great deal from her contact with Miss Patchett, though the evidence is mainly circumstantial. Miss Patchett was a member of a highly reputable Halifax family; her brother was a banker. She seems to have subscribed to local concerts; her name appears as one of the subscribers in Horners' *Views of the Parish of Halifax*. She knew the local gossip, past and present. She was a friend of Miss Anne Lister, of Shibden, and possibly knew the owner of another mansion, High Sunderland Hall.

It is thought most unlikely that Miss Patchett, a known recounter of tales, could have avoided telling Emily the story of Jack Sharp, the builder of Law Hill. He was an adopted nephew of a Mr Walker of Walterclough. He had usurped the two sons of Mr Walker in their father's house and had Walterclough Hall left to him in the old man's will, to rent at a reasonable sum. However, one of the real sons decided to marry and needed a home. He displaced Jack, who built Law Hill overlooking Walterclough, as though threatening it. There was enough in this story to help Emily integrate it into whatever she had heard about the family history from Ireland, and to store it up to form part of *Wuthering Heights*.

The girls educated at Law Hill remembered the school walks very well. One led down from Law Hill towards Brighouse, past a derelict chapel built on a close near the roadside. It had been replaced by a new church named St Anne's, Southowram. Evidence of the state of the chapel in Emily's time is not yet to hand, but it seems likely to have been much like the chapel at Gimmerton, standing in fields and surrounded by old graves. Another walk led through the lower fields to Red Beck, where Emily could see Shibden Hall, being renovated that year. Anne Lister returned from her travels abroad while Emily was teaching. It is most likely that Elizabeth Patchett told Emily about her, and that Emily might have envied her free life-style, but nothing at all can be proved about this.

Mention has been made of High Sunderland Hall, about two or three miles from Law Hill. This extraordinary building was demolished in the early 1950s, but not before a great deal of circumstantial evidence had been collected to show that it was the basis of Wuthering Heights. The layout of the old hall is exactly that of Wuthering Heights; it had the thick walls and buttresses described in the novel: its east chimney would have collapsed into the kitchen if it had been blown down like the one in *Wuthering Heights*; it had a wealth of sculpture, grotesque and pagan, like the shameless little boys featured in the reliefs in the novel; its back was to the north wind, which blows over the brow hungrily. A few hundred yards down the lane from the site of High Sunderland, one can look out for miles at the streets of Halifax suburbs, far below; but they would then have been unbuilt. The windy pathways along which Miss Patchett probably led her energetic girls are still there.

What cannot be proved now is whether Emily could actually see the hall from her window in Law Hill house. She would have had a room on the second floor; the contours of Law Hill and High Sunderland are the same, and Shibden Valley lies between. But a shoulder of Beacon Hill does intervene, so that it is quite impossible to say, now that the old hall is gone, from which part of Law Hill territory it could be seen. It seems very likely that Emily brooded on it and made it her own.

Some other aspects of the Halifax terrain were noted, and later incorporated into *Wuthering Heights*. There is a stone pillar, like the one which pointed the way to Thrushcross, only a few hundred yards from Law Hill, and another was once on the Bradford road. Nearly opposite Law Hill are meadows called Withen Fields, a name which might sound to Emily like 'Withering' or 'Wuthering' fields, though their etymology may be quite different. Shibden is a mansion sheltered by trees and surrounded by cultivated parkland. It became (in the novel) Thrushcross, partly perhaps because along the road there is a hamlet known as Stump Cross. The memory of these names, heard perhaps only once, or not often, emphasises Emily's acute ear.

But the influence of Law Hill went deeper than the suggestion of a terrain for the novel, some words for places, and a pair of contrasting local halls. Miss Patchett was a woman of character. She ran her own life. As well as these energetic and long-remembered walks, she gave the children riding lessons, something which could be a boon to any spirited girl. It might in future give her independence, with the ability to travel about unbeholden to a male escort. It may be significant that one of the rare poems in which Emily mentions horses is dated during the Christmas holiday of the Law Hill employment. Miss Patchett was famous for horses; a mounting block could still be seen in recent years in the yard between schoolroom and house.

Independence, and confidence, began to be breathed into Emily in those six months. Miss Patchett showed her that an independent woman might take a lively interest in the arts. It seems most probable that it was at Miss Patchett's that Emily saw *Fraser's Magazine*, with its heralding, in 1838, of the forthcoming new edition of Shelley's poetry. There seems reason to believe that Shelley had already been one of Emily's favourites. Now she would be able to read the poems in full, when the new edition was available. From this point a Shelleyan tone often replaces the Byronic in Emily's poems. During the Christmas holidays Emily set to work to copy out her existing poems; something had inspired her while at Law Hill, and it seems most rational to suppose that this was a combination of Miss Patchett's personal influence and the literature she may have read there. The four personal poems of November and December 1838 are the most deeply felt so far, though not necessarily the most intense in expression. This too must surely be ascribed to Miss Patchett.

We do not know what caused Emily finally to abandon Law
Hill, probably about March 1839. Homesickness is possible, as
that seems to have been part of the reason for her earlier abandon-
ment of Roe Head. The uneasy balance between the positives of a
new cultural environment and some friendly companionship on
the one hand, and the perpetual round of teaching behind 'my
dungeon bars' must have tipped towards the grinding routine,
and Emily must have been beaten by it. At any rate, she was
presumably home by the time Anne left for Blake Hall in early
April.

Emily's ambivalent attitude to teaching comes out in *Wuthering
Heights*. Some of the sweetest, most attractive scenes are those in
which the younger Catherine guides Hareton's steps on the road
to literacy. The picture of the intermingling hair of the pair, as
they sit in the newly-made flower garden, is affecting and delicate.
Catherine makes a stern taskmistress, but that is because she is
certain of the value of the skill she is teaching. Literacy, at this
point, is everything. We may presume that Emily understood the
subtle feelings flowing between the teacher and the taught; she
may have acquired this knowledge at Law Hill. On the other
hand, the elder Catherine is justifiably scornful of Edgar's liking
for books, especially at crucial times. She rants very effectively,
'Among his books! . . . And I dying! . . . What in the name of all
that feels has he to do with *books*, when I am dying?' If books
were Emily's lifeblood, as suggested by the scene from *Shirley*
where her derivative Miss Keeldar holds tenaciously to hers, it is
interesting that she is able to put the scorn of the raving Catherine
so strongly.

It is impossible to say precisely when the ideas in *Wuthering
Heights* began to crystallise in Emily's mind, but it may seem
possible that some conscious or subconscious story-making was
already in process in the years 1838–9 which would eventually
issue in the great novel. The links between its scenery and
contrasts and the ambience of Southowram and Halifax are too
great to be chance parallels, and they argue either a retentive
memory or a beginning of the story at this point in her life,
though of course it may have been a very different story from the
developed novel, and may have had a nominally Gondal background.

Exactly what Emily did for the following part of 1839 is very
unclear. As both Anne and Charlotte were away from home

during the middle of the year, she must have been much engaged in housekeeping, a pursuit which enabled her to write so accurately of the tasks of her almost-namesake Ellen or Nelly. Quite soon the calm life of the parsonage was to be interrupted by the arrival of a strange and boisterous young man, a new curate, whose character and doings we shall soon need to recount.

None of the Brontës, who all tried educating other children after their own enthusiastically accepted educations, could at first believe the reluctance with which many children allowed themselves to be taught, or the strain this placed on the unfortunate adult entrusted with the task. Charlotte seems to have enjoyed being a pupil at Roe Head, and in 1835 when Anne went there, she worked so conscientiously that in due time she came back with a school prize. Emily disliked being taught, it seems. She lasted only a few weeks at Roe Head before Mr Brontë fetched her home. But in Belgium she would work 'like a horse'. The Brontës wanted to be educated, and they found it hard to believe that intellectual curiosity and artistic expression were faculties left out of some young girls' make up.

Charlotte's longest period of teaching was at the very school where she had been taught, at Roe Head, on the way to Dewsbury. She had been one of Miss Wooler's eccentric but highly intelligent pupils. Now she was invited back as a junior teacher, but there were problems. In 1836 'an unusual degree of stupidity has been displayed by my promising pupils'; in 1838 'I am again at the old business teach – teach – teach.' Again in 1838 'I have been as busy as I could be in finishing up the half-year's lessons, which concluded with a terrible fag in Geographical Problems'. This employment seems to have finished at last in the winter of 1838–9 while Emily was on holiday from Law Hill, and Anne was about to set out for her first unsuccessful attempt to control naughty children, at Blake Hall.[4]

Governesses, not surprisingly, play a large part in the Brontës' books. A deep shock ran through them when they realised how their lives were going to be spent, and their picture of the governess was alternately pitying or scathing according to their degree of self-identification with the current governess of their fictions. Jane Eyre seems the most sympathetic and personably attractive governess, while the sinister Miss Myers in *Wildfell Hall* appears most antagonistically portrayed. Yet we may recall that at one point the three sisters were on the point of running their own school. They had actually printed advertisements, of which copies remain. The parsonage would have made rather a cramped school and occasional encounters with Patrick and Branwell might have alarmed the young ladies. It is often supposed that the Brontës decided to set up such an establishment because there was no alternative unless it was marriage. This may well be the case, but it needs also to be remembered that there was a family tradition of interest in education; Mr Brontë had been an active and innovative teacher and they wished to carry on in his footsteps. In *Wildfell Hall* Anne frequently pinpoints educational discussions.

Charlotte did not stay at home after returning from Miss Wooler's establishment. Within six months she was trying her hand at the lower end of the age range, with education of the small children of Mr William Sidgwick. His house, Stonegappe, was not too far from Haworth, near Cononley on the way to Skipton. Evidence about this episode comes from a member of the family, A. C. Benson, later himself a novelist, whose cousins Charlotte had in her charge. He admitted that Charlotte had been the target of a Bible thrown by one of the children, and that she had disliked being ordered about by the children. In essence, the position was humiliating to Charlotte's fierce pride. She could not endure being in a position halfway between servants and the family, and being able to confide in neither. A well-known anecdote passed on by Mrs Gaskell concerns the occasion when one of the Sidgwick boys said 'I love 'ou, Miss Brontë' and was reprimanded by his mother, who exclaimed in surprise, 'Love the *governess*, my dear!'

Undoubtedly the experience of Stonegappe gnawed at Charlotte's self-confidence. There were two sides to this: the misbehaviour of the children and the disdain of the parents. As Anne shows in *Agnes Grey*, the Brontës were incapable of coping with children who were disinclined to follow their own pattern. We have seen that as children themselves, they were at a complete loss in children's society. They simply could not play ordinary children's games. This lack would surely become acute when faced with childish charges. One also feels, however, that there is an air of superiority about them which partly brought on the children's suspicion. Emily said at Law Hill that she preferred the house dog to her girls. This may have been a joke, but probably not; and this attitude may well have been shown in the faces of all three.

It was not only children that caused Charlotte's despair at Stonegappe. She was expected to carry out many other tasks beyond teaching. Mrs Sidgwick '. . . . overwhelms me with oceans of needlework, yards of cambric to hem, muslin nightcaps to make, and above all things, dolls to dress'. One might have thought Charlotte could have thought of the successive boxes of little toy soldiers, and given the dolls names and adventures, but the effort is beyond her. Piteously she writes to Emily: 'I do not think she likes me at all, because I can't help being shy in such an entirely novel scene, surrounded as I have hitherto been by strange and constantly changing faces.' In short, 'a private governess has no existence, is not considered as a living and rational being except as connected with the wearisome duties she has to fulfil.'[5]

In *Jane Eyre* Charlotte reverses the situation. Though Jane is shy, conscious of her dependence, and physically unobtrusive, she emerges from her silent corner and becomes, in due time, mistress of the house. Yet even before Jane has become a governess, we have the same conflict between a fiery, wilful emotional nexus and the politely dependent image Jane must exhibit. The Lowood scenes are closely based on memory of emotional conflict, and so too are the scenes at Thornfield. The period during which Charlotte served the Sidgwicks taught her the withering contempt in which a governess was held, but it also jolted her acquired Toryism. Blanche Ingram's beauty and finery goes with a mean spirit and uncaring pride.[6] Charlotte was beginning to think, in 1839, that county women might be despicable, though Mr Sidgwick did not earn her condemnation in a like manner; in fact, 'He looked very like what a frank, wealthy, Conservative gentleman ought to be.'

The letter from which these quotations are taken was written to Emily, one of few such that have survived. The tone is a little freer than her tone when writing to Ellen Nussey, perhaps a little more colloquial and excessive. There may be a small element of fellow-feeling in it, for Emily had now given up Law Hill, having had enough of teaching. It is worth remarking that, in *Jane Eyre*, Charlotte gives Jane one single manageable teenage pupil, capable of some rationality; and it may be that Adèle is tinged with qualities adopted from some of the girls that Charlotte met in Brussels.

It was some eighteen months or more after the unfortunate

experiences with the Sidgwick children that Charlotte began looking round once again for a teaching position. In March 1841 she secured one, th $\smile$ time with a family named White, in a house very near to Woodhouse Grove, where her father had first met her mother, so many years ago. This was a few miles from Bradford. Charlotte entered the house with her usual mixed feelings, but her early impression did contain some positive feelings. She had deliberately kept her salary low in order to obtain a place with Mr and Mrs White, whom she considered 'a good sort of people'. The children, once again, seemed 'wild and unbroken', but well disposed; she had some slight misgiving that they might not always remain so.

In her letters to Ellen Nussey, Charlotte's fears and timidity are again on display. She had once again met with children whom she felt incapable of attracting or enthusing: 'I find it hard to repel the rude familiarity of children'. This to some extent gives the game away; Charlotte would have been happier if she could have been on a level with the children, sharing their wildness. She did not feel sufficiently dominant to allow them to joke or play, and thus made no headway. 'But no one', she writes, 'but myself can tell how hard a governess's work is to me – for no one but myself is aware how utterly averse my whole mind and nature are to the employment.'[7] And for Charlotte, as for Emily, nature, whether human or animal kind, and with or without a capital N, was paramount.

As before, it was the lady of the house to whom Charlotte took the dislike. Mrs White seems to have been of a variable temper and accustomed to break into fits of scolding when displeased. She sometimes treated Charlotte as almost an equal, then burst into anger 'in a very coarse unladylike manner'. She little knew that Charlotte was gathering material for high-born ladies for her fiction. However, it was at this house, Upperwood House, Rawdon, that Charlotte found herself attracted to a small child. She nursed the baby and felt at long last that she was beginning to grow rather fond of it. The householder himself, like Mr Sidgwick, did not seem to find such fault with Charlotte. Rochester's quick sympathy for Jane Eyre seems to have had partial parallels.

Later during the year Charlotte's dissatisfaction grew stronger. She seems to have realised that teaching must be her future, but to have wished it could be under her own roof, and with no one but herself and the rest of her family as superiors. She would keep house, just as would Emily, at home at Haworth; but she found keeping house for Mrs White very difficult and could not share her ideas or preferences. Isolated in the midst of company, she liked best the time when the family was away or the children in bed. But the education of children might be tolerable if only the Brontë sisters could run their own establishment. Accordingly, Charlotte began to plan for this. Always it was Charlotte who planned for her sisters, now, and in the attempt to publish their poems, and in the offering to publishers of their novels.

By September 1841, the idea had hardened. The whole family would keep a school. But first they must finish their own education; they badly needed to polish their French and perhaps add German. Mary Taylor, Charlotte's old school friend from her pupil days at Roe Head, knew where such a schooling might be obtained; in due time, the two elder Brontë sisters would sail for Belgium. But before this, there were many preparations to be undertaken.

Though Anne Brontë is not a major subject of this book, her experiences are as likely to have found their way into the works of Charlotte and Emily as they certainly did into her own novels. Her life as a governess began with a short attachment at Blake Hall, following immediately on Emily's return from Law Hill. It is thought that the Ingham family contributed significantly to the characters of the termagants whom Agnes has to discipline, but certainly Anne's report to Charlotte would strengthen her own view, gained through her own experiences with the Sidgwicks and the Whites.

Anne's second encounter with children was at Thorp Green. She began her employment there in 1840 and stayed in the household of the Robinsons for a little over five years, returning to Haworth for holidays, and spending some time at Scarborough. She recommended Branwell to her employers and he joined her at the house in the Vale of York in 1843. Impressions of his tutorship and his relations with the family find their way, changed appropriately, into several Brontë novels. The concern of *Wuthering Heights* and *Wildfell Hall* with the drink problem is in part related to Branwell's addiction, and the degree to which these later Brontë writings, with *Jane Eyre* and *Villette*, develop a critique of Romantic Byronism is affected by the constant presence at Haworth, during the years following mid-1846, of Branwell, bringing with him dissolute habits which had been accentuated by his Thorp Green experiences, whatever they may have been (and details are still far from clear).

At Thorp Green, while Branwell frittered away the goodwill she had initially built up, Anne formed close attachments to the girls in her charge, which were to last beyond her departure from the house. It is not clear why she left in June 1846, but Branwell may have been making life difficult, and besides this the youngest girl had now reached seventeen. These relationships caused Anne to think very carefully about education and tutorship; there may be signs in *Villette* that Charlotte began to share her concern. Charlotte, however, never taught after 1843, except that she seems to have continued her work in the Haworth Sunday school. Here, apparently, she forgot the plea from Jane Eyre that children should be treated as rational individuals with a feeling life of their own. At least one instance was recalled by old scholars of Charlotte humiliating a child almost as severely as the Cowan Bridge teachers. The general impression was 'she was rather hasty tempered'.[8] Emily, it is recorded, never taught in Sunday school, preferring to distance herself from both doctrine and children.

Yet all this presents a strange paradox. The very centre of *Wuthering Heights* is respect for, and marvel at child life. No chapters of *Jane Eyre* are so vivid as those set at Lowood. The children of *Villette* are carefully portrayed and understood. The solution seems to be that Charlotte and Emily wrote as much from memory as from observation, going back to their own deepest childhood feelings when they wanted to describe the minds of child characters. But somehow they were unable to call upon these remembered experiences to help them communicate with real children. In the case of Charlotte, moral doctrine seems to have intervened. Emily guarded herself against close relations with children after 1842, though there are one or two slight indications that she might put casual child visitors to the parsonage at their ease. The Wordsworthian view of childhood affected all the Brontës, but it failed when it clashed with the actual flesh and blood children they encountered as governesses. This does not invalidate their portrayal of children and a balance is achieved by Anne in *Wildfell Hall*, where her good children are not saints and her wicked ones less than devils.

One episode totally unconnected with governess work or educa-

tion must be mentioned here. In 1839, while Anne was away at
Blake Hall and Charlotte much involved after her return from the
Sidgwicks, there appeared in the Haworth firmament the only
young man we know of who added any lustre to the girlhood of
the three sisters. William Weightman was a lively and attractive
new curate, full of charm and teasing good humour, though we
now know that he was mildly deceitful. He succeeded in impress-
ing Mr Brontë and Aunt Elizabeth Branwell and, for a while, the
tone of the conversation in the parsonage seems to have become
skittish.

It seems likely that Anne Brontë became seriously attached to
William Weightman. There seems no other likely explanation of a
series of poems she wrote, including one which was omitted from
the 1846 edition and Charlotte's later selection. His name may
also have been linked with Charlotte's in the gossip between her
and Ellen. Emily alone escaped direct connexion with him, but he
may well have been influential on her writing in two ways. For
the first time, if Anne confided in her, she would have an
example of 'love' close at hand to observe. It may be that the
Romantic affection that Catherine feels for Edgar reflects
Weightman's for Anne, and Edgar's deeper care ‚Anne's for
Weightman.

But possibly the love of Anne for Weightman may have seemed
trivial to Emily. It may have strengthened the strain in *Wuthering
Heights* of Platonic indivisible love, and so helped to intensify
Catherine and Heathcliff. Perhaps some of Lockwood's traits may
have developed from Weightman. But the evidence of Mrs Gaskell
and later writers suggests that there was a degree of genuine
liking in the understanding between all the girls and Weightman.
He alone, of all the Haworth curates, was not cold-shouldered by
Emily, who joined walking parties on the moors with him, though
when other curates were about, she would creep into and out of
any room where they were sitting with lowered eyes and silent
lips.

Charlotte seems to have almost flirted with Weightman for
some while without realising that it was Anne he preferred.
Evidence is very scant indeed, though in February 1840 all the
girls received valentine cards from the curate, posted as far away
as Bradford so that their author couldn't be traced. Charlotte
wrote a cheeky rhyme back. But though Ellen was included in the
quartet to receive valentines, only three titles have survived;

this suggests that one recipient removed hers quite quickly. It could have been Emily, embarrassed and scornful, or it could have been Anne, deeply affected. At any rate, when Charlotte discovered that Anne was especially affected by Weightman's attentions, she did not encourage any further intimacy, it appears. As often with Charlotte's actions and thoughts about Anne, this may suggest some degree of jealousy.

How far this episode affected the novel and poems is uncertain. One can only say that it appears to be the only substantiated case of a real human relationship between a young man and any of the girls before they reached a stage where their characters were fixed. The light-hearted element was paramount, yet the character of Weightman and his flattering ways may have been the basis of a number of characters in all the Brontë novels. The general air of flirtation in the house in the years 1839–42 may have been a factor in the creation of Lockwood's attitude to the younger Catherine, or Rochester's to Jane, whom he teases by the pursuit of Blanche Ingram.

There was very little development in the literary productions of either Charlotte or Branwell during the years 1838–41. Charlotte's short novel *Caroline Vernon*, dating from the early part of this period, was Byronic in tone, with its dashing heroine dazzled by her rakish guardian and eventually becoming his mistress. There was still a great way to go before the firm rejection of Romanticism by Jane Eyre could emerge. Charlotte spent so much time in governess work that she produced very little poetry at this time. Branwell on the other hand wrote a great deal, but it was not improving significantly. His best work was to come in the years ahead when he was emotionally involved at Thorp Green, or trying as best he could to overcome the results of his emotional involvement.

In the early part of the period, Emily made considerable strides in poetry. The year 1839 was one of careful consideration and conscious effort; personal poetry was emerging in front of Gondal fiction. The same change is noticed in Anne's work of 1840. Apart from her venture overseas, Emily had now completed governess work, though the school plan which so excited the family in 1841 would have meant her taking it up again if it had been fulfilled. We sense a deepening of Emily's poetic commitment at this time, and (though hard evidence is lacking) it seems reasonable to suppose some fresh encounter with earlier Romantics. Weightman seems to have played an indirect part. Internal evidence in the poems suggests that in the earlier years of this period Emily had been particularly concerned to develop the Gondal character of 'A.G.A.', the passionate princess with whom she identified.

Governess work, in the end, proved a chore to the three Brontës and they had little personal reward from it. Without it, however, *Jane Eyre* would have been a totally different novel and *Agnes Grey* would hardly exist. Without the interest of relationships between the teacher and the taught, *Shirley* and *Villette* would have been maimed, though these depend more on Belgian experiences. As 1841 advanced, all three sisters became for the moment convinced that teaching, not literature, was the key to their financial future.

7

Belgium

The time Charlotte and Emily spent in Brussels was crucial to the development of both sisters. It was not a happy time. They had an odd position halfway between being pupils and being teachers. It would have been only natural for Charlotte and Emily to have found it strange and demeaning to have to go back to the schoolroom again, and neither of them had much aptitude as teachers. Belgium contributed to the unhappy impression we form of schools and teachers which has been recorded in previous chapters. William Crimsworth, Lucy Snowe, and even the rather pallid Frances Henri win their way to success in their profession, but we cannot help feeling that this success, so clearly desired, was not achieved in real life, and that the disciplinary measures which the two former adopt with their recalcitrant pupils were measures which Charlotte wished she had adopted. There is some evidence for Emily's almost total failure to communicate with her pupils, and Charlotte complains of the bad behaviour of the other girls.[1]

Belgium was a foreign country with an alien religion. Modern readers, used to easy travel and an international youth culture, still feel a mild shock when crossing the Channel. The shock must have been much greater for the sheltered Brontës, whose whole life had been spent in Yorkshire or its immediate vicinity in Protestant communities. In *Wuthering Heights* Nelly Dean is hostile to strangers, by which she means people from different villages, and Joseph is hostile to anyone outside his own strange sect. Emily was more broad-minded than the characters in her novels, but the cultural change for both her and Charlotte must have been immense.

The choice of Belgium rather than France was dictated by a number of random factors. The presence of the Taylors, the cost of living, and greater facilities for learning German all played their part, as Charlotte said in an unusually frank letter to her aunt on 29 September 1841.[2] The object of the journey was to equip

Charlotte and Emily with superior accomplishments in order to qualify them to set up a school. In fact, though both sisters gained immensely from the experience, and Charlotte's whole life was altered, the Belgian qualifications were no help to the Brontës when it came to advertising the school and, unlike Charlotte's heroines, the Brontë sisters did not become successful school teachers.

Mr Brontë and Miss Branwell were, however, persuaded that Charlotte's plan had some merit. Branwell was still in employment as a railway clerk, but did not look like being in a position to support his sisters. Mr Brontë had himself in his youth travelled far to obtain superior qualifications and would appear to have readily fallen in with Charlotte's plans, even to the extent of accompanying them to Brussels, spending some time there and visiting the battlefield of Waterloo, the site of his hero Wellington's triumph.

It was only since 1815 that Belgium had been an independent kingdom. With the population, as now, fairly evenly divided between French and Flemish speakers, French culture predominated. In *The Professor*, Charlotte is fairly scathing about this French culture as exemplified by the loose morals of Monsieur Pelet, and about the intellectual accomplishments of the Flemish speakers. In *Villette* she is contemptuous about the provincial dimness of the Belgian court and the proper names of this novel, Boue-Marine, Lebassecour, and *Villette* itself, reflect this contempt. Homesickness, and a dislike of foreign customs and religion, combined to make Charlotte unusually chauvinistic, although even without these factors it would not be unnatural for an inhabitant of the nation which had defeated Napoleon to feel superior in a country which had hardly begun to feel a national identity.

In using *Villette* and *The Professor* to illustrate what happened to Emily and Charlotte we have to be very careful to distinguish fact and fiction. *The Professor* is set in Brussels, *Villette* is obviously modelled on Brussels. The flat landscape through which Lucy Snowe and William Crimsworth travel is the same as today confronts the voyager from Ostend to Brussels. The cathedral in which Lucy Snowe visits the confessional is recognisably the cathedral in which Charlotte Brontë did the same thing. Not all that much else remains of the picturesque medieval city which Charlotte would have seen, as industrial prosperity soon produced a rash of late Victorian building which in turn is now giving way to modern skyscrapers; but contemporary prints show that the schools on which the action of both novels is sited were situated in very much the same landscape as the schools in which Monsieur and Madame Heger taught.[3] It is the presence of these two schools, situated in close proximity, but separate establishments, which is the most obvious resemblance between fact and fiction.

It is when we turn from places to people that difficulties of identification begin. In *The Professor*, written when the pain of the years in Belgium was still fresh, Charlotte, by making her narrator a man, although one with some obviously feminine traits, was at pains to mask autobiographical elements. Parts of Charlotte's experience enter the character of both Crimsworth and Frances Henri, although the background of the former owes much to an Angrian story about the rivalry of two brothers with an education at Eton thrown in for good measure, while Frances Henri, an orphan like all of Charlotte's heroines, is too insubstantial for us to say much about her. There seems to be no original for M. Pelet, while, if Mademoiselle Reuter owes something to Madame Heger, there is absolutely no evidence for the latter outrageously flirting with two men, as Mademoiselle Reuter does with M. Pelet and Crimsworth.

In *Villette* the resemblances between Madame Beck and Madame Heger are a little closer: we have evidence of the latter's spying and bad faith, at any rate as Charlotte saw them and, in a sense, both Charlotte and Madame Heger were rivals for the affection of Monsieur Heger, as Lucy Snowe and Madame Beck were rivals for the love of Paul Emanuel. Both Paul Emanuel and Monsieur Heger were brilliant teachers and there is a certain amount of evidence in accounts of Monsieur Heger's teaching for that mixture of irascibility and affection which is characteristic of Paul Emanuel. Monsieur Heger would appear to have been a handsome man, happily married to his wife, and his courtesy to Charlotte, although she, starved of affection, may have thought it meant something more, was probably just the polite interest of a good teacher in a promising pupil. Attempts to find models for the other teachers in *Villette*, and pupils like Ginevra Fanshawe and Pauline de Basompierre are probably doomed to failure, although the hot-house atmosphere of jealousy, scandal and gossip that is a feature of the schools in the novels is probably a reflection of real life; these features seem uncomfortably close to the truth to anyone who has taught in such establishments. Lucy Snowe's loneliness in the long vacation would seem to be partly based on Charlotte's feelings in the latter half of her stay, although if we are looking for autobiographical links we must not forget Charlotte's terrible isolation at Haworth during the time *Villette* was composed eight years after she had left Belgium for good.

One important difference between the experiences of Charlotte's heroines and Charlotte herself is that for some of the time she had Emily with her. Lucy Snowe's lonely journey to Belgium, and her adventures in losing her trunk and finding Madame Beck's establishment by chance, are not modelled on reality, since Charlotte travelled to Belgium with her father and Emily and Jo and Mary Taylor. On the second occasion when she went back to Brussels on her own, she travelled by train and was going to a well-established position at the Hegers whom she had known for a year. This obvious difference between fact and fiction ignored by those who like to write the account of the Brontës' Belgian years from the pages of *Villette* and *The Professor*, should make us cautious about using any other source than Charlotte's correspondence in establishing what happened. Unfortunately Charlotte's letters from Belgium were less frequent and more reserved than at other periods of her life.

The decision to go to the Heger establishment in the Rue d'Isabelle does appear to have been almost as fortuitous as Lucy Snowe's arrival at Madame Beck's establishment. In the middle of January 1842 it appeared that the Brontës were destined for Lille. Eventually the British chaplain in Brussels, Mr Jenkins, whose brother lived in Yorkshire, found the Pensionnat Heger. Madame Heger was the proprietor of this school which had about fifty pupils. Her husband taught at the Royal Athenée next door. He had been married before, but had lost his wife in a cholera epidemic in 1833. Madame Heger had inherited the school from her aunt and at the age of thirty-two married, in 1836, Monsieur Heger who was five years her junior. They had six children, whose arrival must have caused some domestic difficulty, although Charlotte was not very sympathetic when the fourth was born shortly after the Brontës' arrival or when the fifth arrived shortly before Charlotte's final unhappy departure. There is no evidence that the marriage was anything but a very happy one.

We have the prospectus of the school. The cost per annum was six hundred and fifty francs, about twenty-five pounds. French, History, Arithmetic, Geography and Writing were taught. Music and foreign languages were voluntary. We learn from Charlotte of visiting masters to teach French, Drawing, Music, Singing, Writing, Arithmetic and German. These supplemented three resident mistresses. There were about forty day-girls and twelve boarders, all of whom, apart from Emily and Charlotte, were Catholics.

This same letter, written in May 1842, speaks of Monsieur Heger as a 'little ugly black being' and mentions, as well as certain difficulties in French, some awkwardnesses between Monsieur Heger and Emily. Charlotte was later to change her mind about Monsieur Heger, and his teaching methods, although exacting, seem to have been extremely successful. The evidence of Charlotte's and Emily's French notebooks show that the girls were encouraged to write free compositions on a variety of subjects, literary, historical and general, and Monsieur Heger's corrections were discerning, careful and encouraging. Some of Emily's essays, particularly that on the Cat and the Butterfly, show the power and originality of *Wuthering Heights*, while Charlotte's essays gain in rhetorical force in the two years she was with the Hegers, although some of the ones composed in her last unhappy months are marred by a certain bitterness. We do not have anything of Emily's before Belgium except a few poems, but Charlotte's prose definitely improves after her two years under Monsieur Heger's tuition.[4]

Loneliness was initially a problem. The Brontës did not get on well with the Jenkins family. The Taylors were at a school at Kockelberg, a long walk away outside the city walls. A day-girl, Laetitia Wheelwright, provided an English link, but she was much younger than the Brontës, as indeed most of the pupils were. The Brontës had each other for company, and M. Heger's lessons must have been stimulating. In May, Charlotte says she is never unhappy and later in the summer reports good academic progress to the extent that the Hegers were now offering them free board and lodging and French and German lessons in return for Charlotte's services as an English teacher and Emily's as a music teacher. There is some unhappiness in this letter concerning the bad behaviour of the other pupils and Charlotte's dislike of Catholicism, but the Brontës' first year in Belgium does not seem to have been particularly distressing. Emily had rarely been happy away from home, but the Hegers do seem to have recognised her worth, and perhaps gave her a much needed boost of confidence.

The deaths in rapid succession of William Weightman and
Martha Taylor cast a sombre note over the autumn, and then Miss
Branwell fell ill, dying before the Brontës had time to come home.
On their return the two sisters bore with them a letter from
Monsieur Heger congratulating them on their excellent progress,
and this was followed by a letter from Madame Heger to Charlotte.
It was decided fairly rapidly that Emily should remain at home to
look after her father while Charlotte should return to Brussels as a
teacher with a small salary. Given Emily's love of home the
decision was probably an easy one, although it may seem unfair.
Anne was away at the Robinsons and had secured a post there for
Branwell. It would have been thought strange for Mr Brontë to
stay on his own at home, and we can dismiss the story of Emily
returning to Haworth to save her father from sinking into drunkenness.[5] There is evidence for Emily being a more unpopular teacher
than Charlotte. The year which Emily did spend by herself
produced some powerful poetry. The experience of Belgium had
widened Emily's knowledge of both French and German literature,
although we do not know how far she was able to carry on her
studies at home; we do have the one tantalising picture of Emily
in the kitchen with a German book in front of her, but do not
know what this book was.[6] Romance suggests some turgid German tale; reality a German grammar.

Charlotte's life is better documented. She left home on 27
January 1843. The journey, like Lucy Snowe's, was an arduous
one but, unlike Lucy, Charlotte travelled by train and Madame
Heger was there, unlike Madame Beck, to receive her with great
kindness in a familiar place. Cousins of the Taylors, the Dixons,
were in Brussels and the friendship with the Wheelwrights was
renewed. The Hegers treated their new teacher in a friendly
fashion, although the salary of sixteen pounds per annum was
low. Charlotte enjoyed giving English lessons to Monsieur
Heger.

Suddenly things started to go wrong. The departure of the
Dixons and the Wheelwrights from Belgium, and Mary Taylor
from Germany, during the course of 1843 deprived Charlotte of
much-needed friends. By 29 May she was reporting that Madame
Heger did not like her, but that she could not understand why
this was so. It was undoubtedly Charlotte's feelings for M. Heger
that caused the rift, although it is hard to explain these feelings,
buried as they are by the veils of Victorian decorum which

confined Charlotte in her correspondence, and the mists of romanticism which she drew over her novels.

Monsieur Heger was an attractive man, interested in Charlotte's
original mind and drawn to her by a common love of literature.
This fact, and Gallic politeness may have overwhelmed Charlotte
who had met few men, most of them being neither intelligent nor
gallant. The curates in *Shirley* are an example of this kind of man.
In loving Monsieur Heger Charlotte was, however, infringing her
own moral code, as Jane Eyre is tempted to infringe hers. It is true
that the heroes of Angria have adulterous affairs by the dozen,
but the teaching of Mr Brontë and Miss Wooler would have
regarded such affairs as immoral, and indeed at Roe Head
Charlotte had been worried by the fascination Angria had for her.
In all Brontë novels, apart from *Wuthering Heights*, adultery is
sternly frowned upon. Branwell's example may have contributed
to this change in attitude from the time of the juvenilia, but
Charlotte's own experiences clearly enter into the reckoning.

Initially Charlotte was slow to recognise her own feelings.
Madame Heger was less slow, and the withdrawal of friendship
which Charlotte found incomprehensible took place by the middle
of the year. Monsieur Heger had stopped taking lessons by 1
May, and while speaking warmly of his kind-heartedness
Charlotte complained bitterly of the want of companionship.
Things got worse. On 6 August Charlotte told Ellen Nussey that
she was in low spirits at the onset of the vacation, when everybody
else would be going home. The terrible long vacation of Lucy
Snowe would seem to be modelled on reality, Charlotte in the
lonely months of 1852 remembering the lonely summer of 1843
including her visit to the confessional which she made on 1
September.

An interesting letter of 1 October, to Emily, compares Charlotte's
isolated position in Brussels to the joys of cooking at Haworth.
Emily apparently thought of herself as idle. Charlotte was reluctant
to come home without a situation to go to, but with the Dixons
and Wheelwrights leaving, Charlotte had no friends in Brussels
and her position with the Hegers was becoming daily more
difficult. On 14 October she scribbled pathetically in her atlas.

'Brussels, Saturday morning, Oct. 14th 1843. First Class. I am
very cold – there is no Fire – I wish I were at home with Papa –
Branwell – Emily – Anne and Tabby – I am tired of being among
foreigners – it is a dreary life – especially as there is only one

person in this house worthy of being liked – also another, who seems like a rosy sugar plum, but I know her to be coloured chalk.'[7]

Before this time Charlotte had given in her notice to Madame Heger, but Monsieur Heger had made her withdraw it. By 19 December she finally decided to come home, and arrived back at Haworth. Though Branwell and Anne were apparently doing well, Mr Brontë's sight was deteriorating. Plans for a school at Haworth proceeded slowly and in fact, though an advertisement was printed offering the usual subjects for thirty-five pounds per annum with French, German, Latin, Music and Drawing as extras for a guinea a quarter, no pupils came to the Misses Brontë's establishment for the Board and Education of a Limited Number of Young Ladies.[8] Meanwhile Charlotte pined for Monsieur Heger.

The story of Charlotte's letters to Monsieur Heger is well known. The existence of any love affair was denied until, nearly sixty years after Charlotte's death, four letters written by Charlotte to her former teacher were discovered. These letters had been, in a rather peculiar fashion, torn up and then stuck together again. On one of them Monsieur Heger had unromantically scribbled the address of his cobbler. Clearly Charlotte wrote more letters than have survived, clearly the correspondence was rather a one-sided one with Monsieur Heger writing coldly or not at all, and equally clearly Charlotte's feelings overstepped the affection pupils sometimes exhibit to their former teachers.

Much else is obscure. We do not know how much Charlotte confided in her sisters. The last letter to Heger is dated 18 November 1845, well after Anne had returned, and the debacle of Branwell's expulsion from the Robinson household had revealed a new and unpleasant side of adultery to the Brontë sisters. They clearly believed that adultery had taken place, and one would have thought Charlotte would be unlikely to have admitted her troubles to Anne, or for that matter to Branwell, if he were sober enough to exchange reciprocal confessions. It is sometimes alleged that Charlotte spoke to Emily who had known Monsieur Heger and who, both in *Wuthering Heights* and her poetry, is at one and the same time compassionate to the sinner and harsh on conventional sanctimoniousness. The evidence for this exchange of confidences is slender. Charlotte in her last letter to Monsieur Heger says that she has denied herself 'absolutely the pleasure of speaking of you – even to Emily', but this may point to polite conversation politely terminated rather than real confessions abruptly ceased.[9]

It is of course possible that both Emily and Anne were aware of their sister's secret, but were too polite or too prudish to mention it. Charlotte's anxious moments of waiting for the postman, even at the six-month intervals, which, cruelly, M. Heger would seem to have settled for as the proper time for communication, would arouse gentle ribaldry, in a modern household. In 1845 she could have excused herself by saying that she was looking for replies to her advertisements about the school, and in 1846 could have claimed she was looking for responses to the publication of the poems of her sisters and herself. Disappointment about the school and about the poems could have masked Monsieur Heger's blighting discouragement. Possibly Emily and Anne knew the truth, but did not dare upset their elder and much loved sister by uttering it. The shadow of Branwell's disgrace fell between Charlotte's return from Belgium in January 1844 and what must have been a final moment of despair following the failure of Monsieur Heger to reply to her letter of 18 November 1845. It is difficult to distinguish between the responses of Emily and Anne to Branwell's affair, squalid and hopeless, but acknowledged and even exaggerated, and Charlotte's heartbreak, pathetic and hopeless, but sternly controlled and repressed.

Charlotte's own responses to her affair can be found in her poems, and her first and last novels. Not all the poems can be dated accurately. Oddly some poems which appear to refer to parted lovers were originally written well before Charlotte left for Belgium. The lines

> Unloved – I love; unwept – I weep
> Grief I restrain – hope I repress
> Vain is this anguish – fixed and deep
> Vainer, desires and dreams of bliss[10]

appear in the poem *Frances*, one of the better poems published in 1846. It might seem to echo very poignantly Charlotte's feelings in 1845 and 1846, as she realised that her love was not reciprocated. The name is of course the same as the heroine of *The Professor*, although the tone is more akin to the dreary anguish of Lucy Snowe in *Villette*. Links with the novels and with biography are rendered less firm, however, by the discovery that lines almost identical to those quoted appear in a much earlier poem, some-times entitled 'Reason', which was almost certainly written before Charlotte went to Belgium. The same is true of 'The Letter' and 'Regret', both of which were definitely first written in 1837. It is possible that when Charlotte first revised her poems in 1843 when she was aware of her affection for Monsieur Heger, and when she revised them for publication in 1845 and 1846 at the time when the smart of her rejection was still felt keenly, she naturally turned to those of her poems which seemed to reflect her present mood. In Belgium and after Belgium, Charlotte felt loneliness as well as love, and poems written at Roe Head reflecting the author's loneliness as well as the love of some Angrian character tied in very well with the mood of 1843 and 1845.

There were, of course, poems having an early origin in which Charlotte more directly reflected her feelings for Monsieur Heger. Three of her better and longer published poems 'Frances', 'Gilbert' and 'Apostasy' are about unhappy love. In the first poem the narrator asks why her lover's eye grew cold and clouded, proud and stern. Charlotte similarly could not understand why Monsieur Heger grew cold and never sent 'word or token', although she must have been rather obtuse not to understand this. In 'Gilbert' we have the story of a man, apparently happily married, who is forced to suicide by the appearance of the ghost of some woman he had previously deserted. This is of course stretching the parallel with Monsieur Heger a bit far, although Charlotte in her more fanciful moments, as we see in her novels, did like to imagine the removal of the inconvenient fact that Monsieur Heger's marriage was, unlike Gilbert's, an entirely guiltless one. In 'Apostasy' we find the two lovers separated by the machinations of the Roman Catholic Church, a theme later developed in *Villette*.

Among unpublished poems we may note 'He saw my heart's woe, discerned my heart's anguish' and 'At first I did attention give' as more naked confessions of Charlotte's love. Both poems may have been written after the publication of *Poems*, but even if written before would have been too frank for publication. Curious-ly Charlotte did use the second poem for publication in *Jane Eyre*, but significantly changed the sexes in such a way that Rochester expresses the lawless love he felt for Jane, the same adulterous love which his creator had felt for her teacher.

The Professor, written very shortly after Belgium, though frequently revised and not published until after Charlotte's death, is another place where a change of sex masks and confuses Charlotte's feelings. Clearly Frances Henri's love, Crimsworth, imagines himself embroiled in an adulterous affair with Mademoiselle Reuter, newly married to Monsieur Pelet (Chapter 20). Since Crimsworth is otherwise coldly virtuous, these lurid daydreams seem incredible and can only be excused by Charlotte's wish both to explore her own adulterous feelings and to examine the possibility that Monsieur Heger might feel torn between a pupil teacher and a successful schoolmistress. The facts that Monsieur Heger was not so torn, and that the successful schoolmistress was his wife, are suppressed.

In *Jane Eyre*, alone in her novels, Charlotte has a hero who is already married. As the poem which Rochester sings shows, some of Charlotte's feelings for Monsieur Heger were transferred to Rochester, an unmasculine although oddly sympathetic figure. Jane's virtue in fleeing Rochester's advances may reflect some of Charlotte's virtuous revulsion at the thought of adultery, just as the rather contrived happy ending may represent the fulfilment of her wishes. In *Shirley* Charlotte, with the success of her first novel, should have been beginning to put Monsieur Heger behind her, although she was unable to resist having two Belgians as heroes, one of them a schoolmaster. In spite of difficulties, the heroines win their way to marrying these Belgians, even though unromantically the cause of these difficulties is not the existence of another wife, but finance and family opposition.

By the time she came to write *Villette*, Charlotte had not heard from Monsieur Heger for seven years, and the triumphs and tragedies of these years should, one would have thought, have driven Belgium out of her mind. But the loneliness of existence at Haworth, and the feeling that she was destined to die without the fulfilment of marriage, brought back memories of 1843 when Charlotte must have realised that she was in love with another woman's husband and could not, unless that woman conveniently died, marry the man she loved. The somewhat bizarre proposal of James Taylor and the still not wholly explored relationship with George Smith confuse the issue, as both characters do enter into the novel, although not as simply as some have maintained. The two years, 1843 and 1852, are curiously blended in *Villette*.

The Belgian landscape is lovingly recalled, although the proper names are disguised. The oppressive atmosphere of the school, smoothly run by the sinister if charming Madame Beck, is authentic, and Lucy's remarks about her are very similar to Charlotte's verdict on Madame Heger. Paul Emanuel is a dynamic if difficult teacher, admired by his pupils and by the general community. Respect for him changes to grudging affection, and this affection turns to love; Charlotte's feelings for Monsieur Heger appear to have followed a similar pattern, although we have no direct evidence about the love. Lucy is separated temporarily from Paul Emanuel by Madame Beck's jealousy and by the claims of Catholic religion. This may be seen as a veiled attempt to portray the rather more serious obstacles that lay between Charlotte and Monsieur Heger, the justified jealousy of his wife, and the restrictions that most forms of religion place between couples, of whom one partner is married to someone else. Fearlessly if rather mysteriously, Charlotte also faced another problem in her life, namely the fact that, though she loved Monsieur Heger, her love was not returned. The portrait of John Graham's not entirely selfless response to Lucy's demand for love may owe as much to Monsieur Heger as it does to George Smith. All three men appear, though good, to have been vain and a little thoughtless about the lame ducks they had encouraged. Only Paul Emanuel is pleased to acknowledge his lame duck turning into a swan.

Adultery in the novel features as prominently in Victorian times as in our times, although attitudes to it have changed. They have changed in the last forty years as they changed in the forty years during which the Brontës lived. Jane Austen, who died two years before Charlotte Brontë was born, is quite contemptuous about Lydia Bennet's 'folly' but accepts fairly briskly the fact that she was in Victorian terms a fallen woman. Thackeray in *The Newcomes* (1855) is very cruel indeed to Lady Clara Pulleyn when she runs away from her brute of a husband, Sir Barnes Newcome to her first love, Lord Highate who despises her, as does the pharisaically virtuous wife of the narrator. Modern readers find Thackeray's attitudes incomprehensible. They are even likely to be surprised by Jane Austen's disapproval of Lydia, in spite of the common-sense it displays, curiously reminiscent of English attitudes in about the year 1950.

Charlotte Brontë and Emily Brontë have a more timeless appeal. Adultery is never condoned. We do not know if it takes place in *Wuthering Heights*. Edgar's feelings are not despised. Nor is the existence of genuine passion denied. The mutual love of Heathcliff and Catherine, and Jane Eyre's feelings for Rochester are lifted on to a more lofty plane than mere convention, a plane which can even be reached by a dull schoolmistress and schoolmaster in Belgium. We do not know what inspired Emily; for Charlotte's inspiration we must be eternally grateful to the two years she spent with the Hegers.

8

Poems

It seems clear enough that one of the major effects on Emily of her stay in Belgium was to direct her attention more firmly to literary composition. A similar effect was noticeable after her 'exile' at Law Hill. Now, returning from M. Heger's influence, and bereft of her two sisters and Branwell, she found herself with time for poetic experiment. It is quite likely that Gondal prose writing also received a fillip in those early months of the first part of 1843, when Charlotte was still across the water and both Anne and Branwell were at Thorp Green, but we are unlikely ever to know any more about that side of Emily's artistic production. Only the poems remain from the Gondal saga. It is certain that Gondal occupied part of Emily's mind in February 1843, when she wrote a lengthy narrative about the fall of Zalona, a city now attacked by Julius Brenzaida, the fierce Gondal monarch who was eventually to be transformed into Heathcliff.

However, the personal poems of this year begin to show development into the kind of thoughtful lyric Emily was to publish some three years later. 'How clear she shines', a poem about the moon, takes its beginning from the actual weather prevailing at the time, as so often with Emily. The moon on 13 April was almost at its fullest; the day had been sunny in part, and a clear sky allowed the filtering of the 'silver' light through Emily's window. (In the 1846 edition the light became 'guardian' light.) In imagination, Emily finds herself transported away from this world which, she says, cannot subdue her entirely. As she gazed into the sky, she brought some degree of specialised astronomical knowledge to the contemplation of the stars above, which she saw as spheres rolling 'In endless bliss through endless years'. Though there is objective evidence of Emily's interest in astronomy as early as 1837, it is likely that she had exchanged views on the matter with M. Heger, who thought she would have become a 'great navigator' had she been born a man.

The poem also has its pessimistic aspect. Although in the far

96

heavens there are worlds where people live in endless bliss, in our own earth it has been the case that:

> ... writhing neath the strokes of Fate
> The mangled wretch was forced to smile;
> To match his patience 'gainst her hate,
> His heart rebellious all the while.

Here, 'Pleasure' leads to 'Wrong' and Joy is 'the shortest path to pain' (this has become the *surest* path in the 1846 edition). Undoubtedly, Emily's understanding had been deepened by her experience in Belgium and was now profiting by a solitude which seemed irksome. Her only companion was her father who taught her to follow his own military habit, practising her in firing a gun at a target set up in the parsonage garden. Meanwhile, she also baked bread and cakes, apparently trying to extend her knowledge of German while doing so. It would be exceedingly useful to know just what German she was reading at this time, for if we knew this we might find whether there is truth in the suspicion that German plots have contributed to *Wuthering Heights*. Even more probably, German Romantic poets such as Novalis may have influenced Emily's poetry.

A relevant question, though not always asked, is how far Anne was responsible for the progress of her sister's poetry. It is, of course, impossible to treat the individual Brontës in isolation. Even without Branwell, their early writings in their home magazines would have had an element missing. Anne was even more closely integrated into the counsels of the other two sisters, in particular Emily. Though Emily had taken the lead in the writing of personal poetry, by dealing with her loneliness in the Law Hill schoolroom, Anne had been the first to treat a more serious theme still, that of her disappointment at the turning aside of the footsteps of a man whom she loved. Later, Anne was apparently to be the first to write a realistic novel, if the references to 'Passages in the Life of an Individual' are really to a first draft of *Agnes Grey*. It is likely that Emily's poems of 1843–4, or at least some of them, were shown to Anne alone.

The two girls had collaborated on Gondal, perhaps from about 1831. They had written joint diary papers in 1834 and 1837, with Emily clearly in the leading role. In 1841 they had written separate diary papers, since Anne was in Scarborough. She was developing a curious habit of dropping Gondal completely as soon as she was out of Emily's sight, and writing her own heart into hymns or other occasional poetry. When the two met again, at Christmas or midsummer, they would collaborate briefly on the Gondal saga. There is particular evidence of this relating to the winter of 1844, and it looks very much as if it was under Anne's influence that Emily began to divide her poems into two exclusive categories, Gondal and non-Gondal. In the 1846 edition of the poems, Anne's work is as well represented as Emily's, and there is some feeling that she may have played a mediating role between her two elder sisters at that time.

The general impression of Anne's work is of tightly written, deeply felt material that breathes sincerity and yet does not quite attract to the extent of Emily's poems. In the poems written between 1840 and 1845 there is perhaps too much self-accusation, a rather narrow field and a certain lack of variety in metre and tone. But in early 1844, and again at the end of the same year, these verses were probably shared with Emily and, since at that point the older sister went on to write some of her best poetry, we must suppose the common effort encouraged both. Though later Anne came to consider Emily's attachment to Gondal dangerous and she seems to have found it impossible to understand Heathcliff's wild destructiveness (Charlotte failed almost as dramatically), during the holidays of the early 1840s, her support of Emily may have been crucial.

One feature is common to much of Anne's poetry and a good deal of Emily's – the internal dialogue. This may well have originated as an external dialogue between the sisters which they carried on alone when they were separated. A typical poem of Emily's using this form is 'The Philosopher' of 3 February 1845. In the manuscript, this is written in such a way as to make clear that there are two speakers, an interlocutor and a 'philosopher' identifiable, broadly, with Emily herself. She wishes to die, so that she will never care 'how rain may steep or snow may cover me'. The interlocutor relates a vision, in which three discordant streams were united by the integrating flash of a marvellous 'Spirit'. The philosopher retorts that she has never been able to catch a glimpse of any such 'Spirit', and adds that if she had done so, the craving to die would not be upon her. This looks like an imagined version of a dialogue which may have originated in a conversation between Emily and Anne (though the sister concerned may have been Charlotte).[1]

It seems quite likely that all the Brontë children had intended eventually to try to see their work into print. Branwell sent poems to *The Halifax Guardian* in 1842, and in doing so was only following in the path of his father. The use by all the girls of copy-books to record edited versions of their poems suggests that they frequently returned to their work with the aim of refining it for publication. There seemed little chance that this would be achieved. It would need capital, of which there was none, and time to arrange the work, yet they were always busy teaching recalcitrant pupils, or preparing to teach.

But when Aunt Elizabeth Branwell died in 1842 she left the three girls a small sum of money each. This was invested in railway shares, which sometimes seem to have been profitable, sometimes not. For a year, Charlotte was abroad in Belgium, then Anne was away at Thorp Green. It was not until mid-1845 that they could discuss this long-term project at leisure. By this time their plan to set up a school had collapsed, yet they knew that one day, when Mr Brontë died, they would be almost destitute. Branwell had become increasingly incapable of surviving himself, let alone of keeping his sisters. During the middle months of 1845, Charlotte must surely have turned over the matter of authorship very often and carefully, though she had not quite given up the idea of the school, or a governess post.

Her opportunity seems to have come in October, when she succeeded in finding one of Emily's copy-books.

> Of course I was not surprised, [she tells us] knowing that she could and did write verse; I looked it over, and something more than surprise seized me, – a deep conviction that these were not common effusions, nor at all like the poetry women generally write. To my ear, they also had a peculiar music – wild, melancholy, and elevating.[2]

This, of course, was written much later, in 1850, when she was presenting the edited remains of her sisters' verse to a public accustomed to the work of the 'Bells'. It is almost sure that Charlotte had expected to find Emily's verse attractive and deep: it is impossible to believe that this was the first time she had seen any of it since the days of the collaboration on Angria. Charlotte held Emily in awe: she had always been considered 'the genius of the family'.

But Charlotte makes it clear that she found it very difficult to persuade Emily to attempt publication. She seems to have enlisted Anne on her side, for though she had less regard for Anne's poetry, she was determined that the work should be a family production. In a trinity of sisters, each girl becomes skilful in playing off one sister against the other. Charlotte was playing for high stakes. For all the family's acute interest in artistic pursuit, Branwell's enthusiasm for painting, the high musical standard reached by Emily's piano playing, and Charlotte's sharp observation so well transformed into clear narrative, almost no financial rewards had been paid to Branwell, and none at all to any of the three sisters. Now, or never, was the time to change all this.

Since it is Emily's poems, or the best of them, which have been judged among the best written in the nineteenth century, Emily's attitude to the matter of publication is of the greatest interest. Evidence has accumulated that despite her clear reluctance to show her work to the world, she eventually participated to some degree in the preparation of the sisters' poetry. Some verbal alterations in the manuscripts which became part of the 1846 text are certainly in her own writing. Charlotte's persuasion evidently had, eventually, a positive outcome.

There was one serious problem to be faced in presenting these poems to the public. All references to Gondal would have to be deleted. In her notebooks begun in 1844, Emily had made a division between personal poems and those related to the Gondal story. But now that an attempt at publication was imminent, she seems to have re-examined the Gondal poems under Charlotte's pressure as well as the non-Gondal, and decided that some of these were fit to be published. It was a Gondal poem, 'The Linnet in the Rocky Dells' which did in fact catch the attention of reviewers the following year. It needed little modification and must have seemed to Emily an obvious choice.[3]

Charlotte's aim seems to have been to present a balanced selection of the poems of all three sisters. There were twenty-one of Emily's, twenty-one of Anne's, and twenty of her own, generally rather longer than those of the others. There is virtually no external evidence about the way in which these poems were edited, or how far the editing was a joint process. Manuscript stanzas were sometimes omitted and additional lines added. For example, Anne's 'Vanitas Vanitatum' gains a four-line section of eighteenth-century feeling, which is not in the manuscript.

Whether it was composed for the published version, or collected from an earlier manuscript now lost, we do not know. A long Gondal poem of Emily's, in which a young captive is set free by a meddling captor, was substantially cut and new lines added, so as to highlight a section where the captive explains that prison life is only tolerable because of the mystic visions which visit her every night.

What is still uncertain, and may never be resolved, is the extent to which Charlotte managed not only the business side of the enterprise, but the selection and revision of the poems. As has been said, there are revisions in Emily's own handwriting. But many revisions appear in the 1846 edition which are not in the manuscripts and there must be a suspicion that Charlotte exerted pressure on her sisters for these changes since, at a later stage, in 1850, when she came to edit their poems after both sisters were dead, Charlotte altered them radically. However, we should not underestimate Emily's habit of perpetual revision; for where we have multiple manuscript copies of her poems, they show that she almost always made minor alterations, however long it was since the poem had first been composed. Anne also revised in a similar way.

Charlotte had not chosen a good time to launch the Brontës' poems. For some time she seems to have cast about among publishers who were finding it hard to make ends meet; for there had been a considerable change since the days of the Romantics. In the end she wrote to Chambers, whose *Journal* was among those the Brontës read from time to time (it is not known whether they actually bought it by this date). Their advice was to contact Aylott and Jones, who might publish if the authors would be prepared to undertake the cost themselves. Nowadays such publishing is called 'vanity' publishing and frequently despised. It does not seem that Charlotte had any scruples about moving to this form of publication. Though it turned out at first to be financially unprofitable, it is likely that the sisters gained confidence by seeing themselves in print. Quite certainly they learnt a great deal about the mechanics of English. Emily began to understand the I before E rule for the first time, and all the sisters became aware of the elementary rules of punctuation.[4]

A thousand copies of the volume by three unknowns called 'Bell', simply entitled *Poems*, were printed. It would be of great interest to discover the manuscript from which the printed text was set up. At this distance, it seems unlikely that it will ever be found and we may only speculate on whether it was written by Charlotte alone, who may thus have had the final veto on anything appearing in the printed version, or by each of the three sisters, as A. M. F. Robinson says. Review copies of the work were available by 25 May 1846, and the book seems likely to have been on sale by the end of May. It was issued under the pseudonyms which the sisters had agreed on; Charlotte was known as 'Currer', Emily as 'Ellis', and Anne as 'Acton'. The origin of these names is disputed and, indeed, they may have arisen from many sources combined. However, we do know that it was the intention of the three not to identify their sex; this was, in fact, disputed by reviewers and the public until after Emily's death, when Charlotte felt free to announce their real names.

It turned out that the caution of various publishers in issuing this new volume of poems was entirely justified. Despite some favourable reviews to which we shall shortly return, the books failed almost completely to sell. It is well known that over a year later Charlotte was compelled to admit that only two copies had been bought. This might have seemed a disaster, except that the novels were by now the Brontës' major concern. Authorship was proving a struggle, but it must seem that even this limited venture into print had provoked the sisters to carry on enthusiastically. They had crossed the divide between unpublished authors and published ones.

Some time during the winter of 1845–6, during which the poems were being edited and copied, there seems to have been a breakdown of relations between the sisters. This may have been in part brought on by Branwell, who, since his dismissal from the employ of the Robinsons, had been distraught and disconsolate, and was increasingly turning to drink as the anodyne for his condition. From now until his death in late summer 1848, he was rarely in total command of his faculties and seems to have been the cause of anguish to his father and great worry to his sisters. It is said that Charlotte refused to speak to him, and it may be that her attitude was one cause of the dissension mentioned: Branwell was exceedingly taxing; on one occasion he set his bed on fire and it has been alleged that this may be one origin of the frightening scene in *Jane Eyre* where Bertha tries to kill Jane in the same way.

The clearest indication of the tense atmosphere of early 1846 comes in Anne's poem 'Domestic Peace', which Charlotte modified and entitled in her 1850 additions to the 1846 poems. In the final stanza Anne clearly indicates that the arguments were set off by the whole family, not Branwell only; and it is at this point that different viewpoints emerge in the work of Anne and Emily. It seems likely that the process of editing and submitting to publishers was a highly contentious one. It may be that the omission of Branwell from the trio was disputed by Emily at least, but Charlotte held firm in excluding him.

This spirit of dissension does not, of course, appear prominently – if at all – in the 1846 selection. It had advanced too far for these disagreements to have any effect on it. But on the work to come, in *Wuthering Heights*, *Jane Eyre* and *Wildfell Hall*, and in Anne's late poems, Branwell's disruptive behaviour would be reflected. Part of the great advance these novels and poems make on the juvenilia is to be ascribed to the shattering experience of coping with Branwell's debility and ineffectiveness; the results of too close an allegiance to Byronic Romanticism were seen and felt to the full.

Emily's poems were, of course, the gems of the 1846 collection. Of the three sisters, she alone has stood the test of time as a poet and produced work of a standard to be placed alongside the greatest English poetry. The twenty-one poems printed in 1846 include several which have been subsequently anthologised, memorised, set to music and analysed by critics. Among these are 'Stars', 'The Philosopher', 'Cold in the Earth' and 'The Linnet in the Rocky Dells'. The manuscripts of these and the others chosen by Charlotte and Emily as they looked through her work that autumn are copy-books, divided in an 1844 copying into Gondal and non-Gondal poetry. The two sisters now began to carry out a process of de-Gondalising the fictional work, which would make no sense to the public without their Gondal context.

Even the non-Gondal poems were revised. This process was only a continuation of Emily's normal practice, shown by her remaining manuscripts. She did not abandon a poem once written, but would come back to it at intervals to alter and modify it, sometimes recasting it completely and welding it into a longer narrative. Now that the 1846 edition was in prospect, she looked carefully over the two copy-books, and began to alter the poems carefully. Apart from de-Gondalising, she changed words which appeared repetitious or confusing, and sometimes seems to have toned down unusual or baffling phrases, a process which Charlotte carried much further in the 1850 posthumous edition and which is perpetuated even in modern editions.

Emily's poems were not startlingly innovative. Metrically they were varied and derived from a number of exemplars which we have already mentioned. There has seemed to some critics to be a felicity in her choice of metres and the generally simple language used. The vocabulary was indeed relatively easy to understand; there were few unusual or extremely literary words. In these matters Emily seems to have followed the less grandiloquent eighteenth-century writers such as Cowper and the hymn writers. The dialect words so frequent in *Wuthering Heights* made no appearance in the 1846 edition, though a few are present in poems published since.

Nor were there any startlingly new topics in the poems of 'Ellis Bell'. Most were quietly ruminative, idyllic and descriptive. Nature was present, but not the detailed naturalistic descriptions of Clare. Emily's sensitivity to weather conditions, dating back to the day of the bog burst or before, provides her reader with almost a landscape approach to poetry. Sun, rain, wind, the cold earth, golden evenings are the background to melancholy partings and dialogues. The sense of loss, of a loss of paradise, is Wordsworthian. The speaker of the poems is generalised, not specific. It is not always clear whether a man or a woman is reciting. But the poems do seem to be recited; they seem to be auditory poems, in which a quiet melodious voice talks insistently.

The emotional tone of Emily's poems is not so high pitched as the tone of *Wuthering Heights*. Death provokes grief, loneliness, gentle hope, (which, however, 'Went, and ne'er returned again' in the poem called 'Hope'). The most vivid is perhaps the very-much-edited 'The Prisoner: A Fragment', in which Emily describes the unearthly visitation of a female captive, whose consolation is to be wrapt into a trance at evening with the 'Western winds'. The direction of the wind in this and other poems may significantly remind us of Shelley.

It is on this poem that Emily's reputation for mysticism depends. Argument has raged on the question of whether she was a 'mystic', though definitions of the term have been rare. If we seek to show that Emily believed passionately in the power of imagination, as did her mentors among the Romantics, many poems, if we trust their prose significance, would seem to show this. In

Shirley Charlotte seems to suggest more; that her sister (if Shirley Keeldar is truly modelled on her) entered mystic trances in the presence of some types of natural phenomena. The central portion of 'The Prisoner' lends credence to this impression.[5]

Yet, of course, we have very little external evidence for Emily's trances, if she did in fact undergo them. The poems were not written without intense emotional experience and Emily could not always command her poetic gift. The 'visitant' which Charlotte specifies in a later addition to a part of the same poem, and the 'messenger' which the captive entertains in Emily's original, are vague concepts; the interpretation of either must remain disputed. Who can say whether these poetic entities qualify the poet for the title of 'mystic'? Clearly, Emily's underlying and deeply held belief is transcendental, but that we should have expected from all her heritage and childhood experiences.

Since the 1846 edition, many more of Emily's poems have been printed. The general effect of this has been to widen the range, but not to deepen the feeling of her work. A number of narrative poems are now known, placing a Byronic importance on armed men escaping from pursuers, on strife between kindred, on the heroism and pain of war, and the exploration of desolate country by lonely wanderers. There are now many more lyrics, with numbers of part-finished poems and poems which were never intended to be finished. It becomes clear that Emily Brontë would write down couplets and individual lines as a matter of course, without knowing where they might lead; she frequently tried to finish off the poem later, not always with success.

Charlotte's 1846 poems were, on the whole, longer than those of the other two and for that reason there were only twenty instead of twenty-one. The best reflect Charlotte's own experiences as a teacher, or as an exile of some sort away from home. We may perhaps see signs of *Jane Eyre* in some of these; the loneliness of a governess, her dependence and fretfulness under restraint were all emotions known to Charlotte, expressed in her poems and then re-visited in *Jane Eyre*. A few of these poems too had fictional backgrounds deriving from Angria but, like Emily, Charlotte toned down or removed the fictional elements.

Anne's poetry may well have been included in the collection purely from sisterly feeling. But some of the poems of 'Acton Bell' stand up well to re-reading; for example, 'Home', though simple, is exceedingly well crafted and expresses very carefully the emotions it carries. Like Emily, Anne had been refining her poetry over the years. On the whole the poems are taken from the most recent copy-books, just as in the case of Emily. Some of the poems differ from those of the other two by reason of their explicitly religious themes.

The poems of all three sisters, like their subsequent prose work, bear a family resemblance. Their topics have a homogeneity, and their verse forms, so often taken from their late eighteenth-century masters, are often the same. Uncluttered sentences, straightforward vocabulary, conventional poetic word order are found in the poems of all three (as in those of Branwell, which was not included). The sisters did not make any attempt at radical innovation, apparently taking the view that poetic form was a ready-made bottle into which their home-brewed ale might be poured.

Critical reactions to the edition were mixed, but not discouraging. The *Critic*, for example, said 'it is a long time since we have enjoyed a volume of such genuine poetry as this'. Its reviewer described the small book as a ray of sunshine, 'gladdening the eye with present glory, and the heart with promise of bright hours in store. Here we have good, wholesome, refreshing, vigorous poetry ...' Among Emily's poems particularly praised was 'The Linnet in the Rocky Dells', originally a Gondal funeral song, perhaps written as the final word on 'A.G.A.', the Gondal heroine with whom Emily in part identified. Charlotte's poem 'The Letter' was also praised.[6]

The *Athenaeum* chose the volume as one in which 'appears to run the instinct of song'. The reviewer had come near to the truth. Had he seen the Brontë family gathered round the cottage piano on a winter's evening, playing and singing Moore's songs, with their distant echoes of the ballads sung in Mr Brontë's childhood, he would have realised where that 'instinct' came from. He chose Emily's poems as the most inspired, with 'a fine quaint spirit .... and an evident power of wing that may reach heights not here attempted'. Charlotte's poems also gained his approbation, but he confirmed Charlotte in her view of Anne's inferiority, by suggesting that she needed the 'indulgences of affection'.

Best of all the early reviews was an unsigned article in the *Dublin University Magazine*. The writer traced one of the sources of the 'Bells'' poetry, naming 'a sort of Cowperian amiability and sweetness, no-wise unfragrant to our critical nostrils' as the 'uniform tone' of the poems. Among Emily's poems he selected 'Stars', and 'O Day! He cannot die' ('A Death Scene'). Charlotte's 'Gilbert' and Anne's 'A Reminiscence' were also chosen for quotation. The verses were praised for their 'unobtrusive feeling' and their 'unaffected and sincere' tone.

These generally cheering reviews did not have much effect on the sales of the book, but they do seem to have encouraged the three poets. There was undoubtedly much more poetry to come from each pen, but all three soon became diverted into novel writing. Charlotte wrote only a few more lines of verse after this, and Emily only two more poems. Anne seemed to be just reaching her poetic capacity; she had more to write in 1847–9. Yet all these budding poets changed course and soon emerged as writers of what Charlotte modestly called 'prose tales'; the verse narrative tradition exemplified by Byron and Scott had borne fruit in the work of all the sisters. But on the whole these poems were not selected for the 1846 edition.

It may be worthwhile at this point to consider the role of the publication of the poems in furthering the artistic development of the three Brontë sisters and to raise the matter of their change of direction. An examination of the poem manuscripts of Emily and Charlotte show that, before their entry into the world of publication, they were ignorant of or disregarded quite common conventions of English writing. For example, punctuation in some of these manuscripts, right through their adolescence, is rudimentary. Emily's poems, even in the 1844 copy-books, use full stops and dashes as equivalents. Commas are rather rare and there is inconsistency in their use. Anne appears to have added some punctuation en bloc after copying out some of the poems, and there are traces of similar practice in Emily's work. We have to conclude that until faced with the need to produce conventionalised final copies, they cared little about punctuation.

The spelling conventions of all four Brontës were far from standard before 1846. Both Branwell and Emily disregarded the I before E rule, and there are examples in their work and in Anne's of eighteenth-century spelling lingering on. Those compositions of Anne and Emily, produced or copied after the 1846 edition was published, are greatly changed. It seems that the need to order their poems and to correct proofs, may have been a necessary stage in grasping the need for conventional mechanics of English. While even Charlotte's novel manuscripts, which have survived, show some similar eccentricities, it is possible that without the discipline of correcting poem proofs, they might not have made a good impression on any publisher to whom they sent their work.

Charlotte wrote much less poetry in the 1840s than her sisters. In part this was probably due to her occupation in Belgium, which lasted so much longer than Emily's. But it may be that already Charlotte was beginning to feel herself more a novelist than a poet. Anne's continued practice of poetry up until her death in 1849 shows that she considered herself as much a poet as a writer of fiction, though the public will hardly agree. Emily seems to have worked out her eternal themes in whatever medium came to hand. The Gondal poems appear to be interluded within the general Gondal epic, and often deal with similar material to that of *Wuthering Heights*.

It appears that the three sisters had decided to submit a novel each before they knew the fate of the poems. They did not wait, find out that the poems would not sell, and *then* write novels; they changed their direction before sales of the poems were confirmed and then (except for Anne) largely abandoned poetry. This argues a common decision, perhaps influenced by Charlotte, who may even have been influenced by considerations of publishability. As we can see looking back, the change of direction was a vital one, destined to fulfil the ambitions and yearnings of all three sisters; but in 1845–6 it may have been very hard to discern the benefits it might bring. If the Brontë poems are overshadowed today, we should at least think of them as a most important training ground for Charlotte, and a genuinely artistic medium in the hands of Emily and Anne.

9

Jane Eyre and *Wuthering Heights*

We know a good deal about the publication of the Brontë novels, but we know little about their composition. On 6 April 1846 Charlotte wrote to Aylott and Jones saying that the three Bells were preparing for press three distinct and unconnected tales, to be published either separately or as a three-volume novel. Aylott and Jones indicated that they were not publishers of fiction, and recommended other publishers. On 4 July 1846 she wrote to Henry Colburn asking him for permission to send three tales to him. These three tales were *Agnes Grey*, *The Professor* and *Wuthering Heights*. The manuscript of *The Professor* is dated 27 June. There is no way in which we can date the inception of the novels. Anne mentions 'Passages from the Life of An Individual' in her diary paper, dated 30 July 1845, but though this could be an apt description of *Agnes Grey*, it could refer to some other narrative. The winter of 1845 to 1846 was a very cold one and may have suggested the opening scenes of *Wuthering Heights*, but this is a very slender piece of evidence for the composition of *Wuthering Heights* which may have been begun much earlier. There is a story of Branwell reading a manuscript which his friends remembered as being like *Wuthering Heights* as early as 1841. The story is a dubious one, and the inference that Branwell was partly responsible for *Wuthering Heights* is still more dubious but, apart from her poems, Emily did not have a great deal to do in the years 1843 and 1844.

It is unlikely that the manuscript of *Agnes Grey* underwent any revisions between submission and publication. *The Professor* was not published until after Charlotte's death and underwent substantial revisions as Charlotte tinkered with it several times, especially in 1851, before embarking upon *Villette*. It is still, like *Agnes Grey*, a short novel, whereas *Wuthering Heights* is much longer. It is therefore quite likely that at some stage in 1846 Emily may have lengthened her novel in order to accommodate *Wuthering Heights* and *Agnes Grey* into a three-decker novel. The fact that Emily has left no poetry surviving written in this period is perhaps a further indication that she was revising and lengthening her work, although it is very hard to see how *Wuthering Heights*, seemingly so integrated a work in spite of its shifts of mood and narrator and generation, could have existed in a shorter form.[1]

The three works were sent to various publishers who rejected them. We do not know when and why it was decided that *The Professor* should go its separate way. At first sight, as a novel about teaching, it has more in common with *Agnes Grey* than the latter has with *Wuthering Heights*. Our best account of the publication of all three novels comes from Charlotte Brontë's biographical notice, printed in the second edition of *Wuthering Heights* and *Agnes Grey* after Anne and Emily had died. Any disagreements between the three sisters are likely to have been minimised in this pious memorial.

The not very efficient or honourable firm of Thomas Newby and Son accepted *Agnes Grey* and *Wuthering Heights* at some time in the middle of 1847. Charlotte complained of the terms they offered, and of their slowness in seeing the book through the press. It is unlikely that it was Newby or his terms that precipitated the decision to exclude *The Professor* since, when Charlotte sent her manuscript to the firm of Smith, Elder and Company, it was noted that the envelope, economically but naively, had on it the names of three or four publishers who had rejected it. This would suggest that *The Professor* had been on its own for some time before it went to Smith, Elder on 15 July 1847.

Students of the Brontës owe a great deal to the firm of Smith, Elder. The proprietor George Smith, a young man of immense energy, rescued the firm from insolvency and at the end of his long life it had become a famous part of Victorian England. His reader, W. S. Williams, a quieter and more pathetic figure, was the person who wrote the original letter commending *The Professor*, and saying that a three-volume novel would receive considerable attention. Both men looked after the Brontës very well, before and after the deaths of Emily and Anne. The tact of Williams and the energy of Smith were a good combination. The Brontës cannot have been easy to deal with and George Smith was occasionally insensitive in not recognising how vulnerable they were, but he made no mistake with *Jane Eyre*.

Jane Eyre is supposed to have been begun in August 1846 when Mr Brontë was being operated on for cataract in Manchester.[2] When Charlotte received the reply from W. S. Williams she had almost completed it and his kindness acted as a spur. She finished the manuscript on 19 August, and sent it off on 24 August. George Smith read it at a sitting and publication was rapid. The novel was published on 19 October and was an immediate success.

There are obvious autobiographical features in *Jane Eyre*. Charlotte herself claimed resemblances between Cowan Bridge and Lowood, she had been a downtrodden governess, Mr Rochester, married and masterful, is like Monsieur Heger, Moor End is like Hathersage where lived Henry Nussey, a clergyman who had proposed marriage to Charlotte, as St John Rivers proposes to Jane, and the mysterious voice of Rochester which calls away Jane from this marriage was said by Charlotte to be based on a real incident, although it is hard to see what. Drunkenness in the shape of Bertha Mason and Grace Poole, and Mr Rochester's blindness, have less direct links with the condition of Branwell and Mr Brontë. The happy ending, perhaps rather hurried, to a novel full of suffering perhaps reflects Charlotte's joy at the good news from Smith, Elder after so many disappointments.

We have in this last instance shown how wrong it is to make autobiographical equations too exact. Mr Brocklehurst was a hypocrite, Carus Wilson probably was sincere. Jane Eyre goes to Lowood alone in disgrace, but Charlotte Brontë was with her sisters. Henry Nussey had none of St John Rivers' high heroic qualities. Finally and most oddly, though Mr Rochester has something of Monsieur Heger's attractiveness, he also has something of Charlotte Brontë about him.

Charlotte's novel had already received rapturous reviews and some financial reward by the time *Wuthering Heights* and *Agnes Grey* were produced. Little is known of Thomas Newby but what is known does not redound to his credit. His publishing business does not seem to have lasted long and we know of no other famous novelists whom he published. Anne and Emily would seem to have paid him fifty pounds for the privilege of having their novels published, and not to have recovered all this sum. The novels took a long time to publish and when published were full of errors. We do not have the manuscript of *Wuthering Heights*, and Emily may not have been a good proof reader, but a first edition of Wuthering Heights makes difficult reading because of the way the printer has split up paragraphs into short sentences as a way of making the book seem longer than it is.[3] Some of Charlotte's corrections in the second edition are insensitive, but her hostility to Newby was fully founded. As well as being incompetent, Newby was clearly dishonest since, when Currer Bell's work was a success, he did not hesitate to advertise the works of Ellis and Acton as being by the same author.

This was in a way counter-productive since, so far from the good reputation of *Jane Eyre* helping to sell the novels of Newby, the reputation of *Wuthering Heights* for coarseness helped to damn *Jane Eyre* for the same fault. The tendency to assume that all the Bells were one and the same, and that they were a bad lot, became marked in 1848 when *Wildfell Hall* was published and was condemned for its shocking sentiments. Since Helen Huntingdon, the heroine of this novel, behaves as does Jane Eyre with exemplary rectitude, these attacks seem very unfair, especially as it would seem that Anne's second novel is in some respects a counterblast to Emily's.[4]

We would like to know more about the publication of all three first novels and about how the Brontës reacted to them, since the circumstances surrounding the reception of a first novel is clearly likely to affect the writing of the second. One of the difficulties about charting the story of the Brontë novels is remembering the inevitable gap that must occur between the inception of a novel, its publication and its reception by reviewers. Thus most of *Jane Eyre* was written at a time when the *Poems* were not selling and *The Professor* was being constantly rejected. *Agnes Grey* and *The Professor* were written before this time, as was all or part of *Wuthering Heights*. Anne Brontë's second novel was being written at the time of the good reception of *Jane Eyre* and poor reception of *Wuthering Heights*, and this fact, as well as a genuine concern with the morality of Emily's novel may have influenced Anne. We do not know when *Shirley* was begun. This novel will be discussed in the next chapter. Its cheerful opening clearly reflects the happy circumstances in which Charlotte found herself in the opening months of 1848 after the success of her first novels. The year was one of revolution abroad and threatened insurrection by the Chartists at home. In taking as her subject an earlier revolution at the time of a foreign war, Charlotte is showing the concerns of her age, although her reluctance to enter the public rather than the private sphere is shown by her setting this novel in a previous generation.

Wuthering Heights is also set in a previous generation. In it, instinctively rather than by historical research, Emily charts the decline of the Yorkshire working farms in favour of the new industrial society which grew up at the beginning of the nineteenth century.[5] It would be a mistake to reduce the novel to this narrow sociological base, but the conflict between Wuthering Heights and Thrushcross Grange, and the move to the latter by Hareton and Cathy at the end, do suggest what was happening all over Yorkshire in the nineteenth century. By the time Mrs Gaskell wrote her famous account of the West Riding of Yorkshire, households like Heathcliff's were clearly the exception rather than the rule, although she gives clear evidence that *Wuthering Heights* was founded on reality.

Still there are those remaining of this class – dwellers in the lonely houses far away in the upland districts – even in the present day – who sufficiently indicate what strange eccentricity, what wild strength of will, nay, even what unnatural power of crime, was fostered by a mode of living in which a man seldom met his fellows and where public opinion was only a distant and inarticulate echo of some clearer voice sounding behind the sweeping horizon.[6]

Reading contemporary reviews of the Brontë novels is a depressing business. The English literary critical factories did not exist and reviewers were amateurs who tended to concentrate on content rather than style, quoting in addition large sections of the novels in order to give their readers a flavour of what they might expect. Modern students of the Brontës, devoid of original ideas on what to say about *Wuthering Heights* and *Jane Eyre*, sometimes make the mistake of turning to these reviews for inspiration. It is not helpful to say, as one reviewer did, that the moral of *Wuthering Heights* is that it shows what Satan could do with the law of Entail. Another reviewer claimed that *Wuthering Heights* had two heroes, Edgar Linton and Heathcliff.[7] Others more perceptively saw that Emily was reluctant to condemn Heathcliff and were baffled by this reluctance. *Jane Eyre* was originally praised for its freshness, but later reviewers, linking this novel with *Wuthering Heights*, and even more with *Wildfell Hall*, objected to the coarseness of the Bells. The famous objections to Jane Eyre's character made by Lady Eastlake in *The Quarterly Review* of December 1848 to the effect that 'almost every word that she utters offends us', deeply wounded Charlotte, in some distress at this time, and she made the mistake of trying to answer the objections in *Shirley*.

Both contemporary praise and contemporary blame should not be taken too seriously when considering the real merits of *Wuthering Heights* and *Jane Eyre*. It is a useful reminder of the vanity of contemporary judgements to read in the same journals that damned the Brontës, either with faint praise or with loud condemnations, reviews of totally forgotten novels that are full of eulogies about high moral and artistic standards. The failure of the Brontës to live up to these standards can be explained by their isolation which had often forced them into reading books of a previous generation or from a foreign culture. The fact that *Jane Eyre*, and to some extent *Wuthering Heights*, definitely have remained popular with all cultures and all generations is a tribute to that universal appeal which is the hallmark of great art. The many who praised *Jane Eyre* and the few who praised *Wuthering Heights* in 1847 and 1848 were discerning enough to see that their greatness lay in the ability of their authors to step right outside the conventions of the day.

Thus in considering the Brontës' two best-known novels it is not particularly helpful to know contemporary attitudes, since they so clearly rejected them. It is however worth considering two particular aspects of the Brontës' works which particularly offended the likes of Lady Eastlake, since in these matters Charlotte and Emily did in a way reflect as well as reject the prejudices of the time.[8]

Class divisions are conspicuous in both novels. They are even more conspicuous in *Agnes Grey* where Agnes Grey's father is a poor clergyman despised for his lack of money, but clearly thought superior by Agnes and her mother to the rich but vulgar Bloomfields who are Agnes's first employers. Jane Eyre has a similar parentage, but turns out via the Rivers family to be just as grand if not as rich as the vulgar Reeds. She is snobbishly condescending to the poor girls she teaches at Morton and snobbishly appreciative of the aristocratic lineage of the aristocratic sounding Edward Fairfax Rochester and St John Rivers. We remember awkwardly Mr Brontë's arrogance about his name and ancestry, Charlotte's rude remarks about her vulgar employers, the Whites, her inability to appreciate the working classes in *Shirley*, and rather paradoxically her contempt for the provincial aristocrats in *Villette*. All this goes against our sympathy for Jane as a symbol of the downtrodden classes fighting her way through life by the strength of her own personality, and against the condemnations of the reviewers of 1848 who saw *Jane Eyre* as a revolutionary book in that year of revolutions.

Even more baffling contradictions are thrown up in *Wuthering Heights* where much of our sympathy towards Heathcliff at the beginning of the novel stems from the fact that Hindley oppresses him and Catherine is prevented from marrying him by reason of this degradation and the superficial attraction of Edgar Linton's superior rank. Much of the feeling we have that Wuthering Heights is somehow better than Thrushcross Grange, in spite of its harsh climate and the wild ways of its inhabitants, is due to the way in which Emily presents one house as an organic whole with master mucking in with man and maidservant, while the other is full of artificial distinctions between servants and their superiors. On the other hand, Heathcliff as a symbol of the oppressed does not really work, since in his three years' absence he acquires the manners and the means of a gentleman, and thereafter acts as an oppressor. Indeed attempts to show Heathcliff as a representative of the proletariat ignore the fact that he begins the novel and ends his life as a typical capitalist owning one house and renting another. Hareton Earnshaw too is an unlikely symbol of the downtrodden poor since he, too, ends up by owning two houses, and some stress is laid on his ancient lineage since he bears the same name as the Hareton Earnshaw who lived in Wuthering Heights in the year 1500.

The Brontë family's social status was a peculiar one. The clergy were gentry, and in Haworth there was little opportunity to mix with ordinary people, but also little opportunity to mix with other members of the gentry. Mr Brontë's peculiar ancestry, the death of Mrs Brontë, the absence of any nearby relatives, the backwardness of Haworth, and the relative poverty of the living there meant that the Brontës had very few friends in any class. Their experiences as governesses and in Belgium made them resentful of any patronising claims to superiority, and this feeling of wounded pride comes through in many of the novels. Hunsden Yorke Hunsden in *The Professor* is a mass of contradictions, proud of his ancestry, but contemptuous of the aristocracy, and we find the same confusion in his creator. The presence in the North of England of a new class growing wealthy from industry does not have a particular impact on the novels, but odd characters like the Bloomfields in *Agnes Grey*, Sam Wynne in *Shirley* and the Watsons in *Villette* show the Brontës' attitude to this class.

Other novelists of the nineteenth century give a more consistent picture. Jane Austen satirises snobbery in Lady Catherine de Burgh and Sir Walter Elliott, although she is fairly cruel with pretentious upstarts like Mrs Elton. Thackeray, who gave the term snob its present sense, is fairly skilful in depicting the foibles of mankind in this respect. George Eliot, from a less elevated position than either of the two previous authors, but with a very wide range of knowledge, is able to paint in *Middlemarch* a good picture of the social structure of England with each class on speaking terms with the one immediately above and below it, while Mrs Gaskell is, in novels like *Mary Barton* and *North and South*, able to portray sympathetically the workers and the factory owners whom Charlotte treats so unsympathetically. Nobody could really say that the Brontës had any very useful or consistent message to give about the position of the classes in Victorian England, although today the confusion of these classes and our confused attitude to them makes this failure unimportant.

More important in people's eyes today, and even more shocking in contemporary eyes, were the Brontës' views on the relations between the sexes. Prudery like snobbery is a complicated subject with rapid changes in attitudes taking place within a very short time. The Brontës were considered shocking and coarse probably because they were unaware of English Victorian standards, having done so much of their reading among foreign authors or authors of a previous generation. We can find little to be shocked at, although we can perhaps see why *Jane Eyre*, *Wuthering Heights* and *Wildfell Hall* caused a few eyebrows to be raised. Sexual passion, albeit usually delicately phrased and, except in the rather odd case of *Wuthering Heights*, kept within the confines of morality, is dealt with honestly by the Brontës. This is in contrast to Jane Austen where social rather than sexual reasons seem to determine marriage except for a few unfortunate cases like Wickham and Willoughby. Thackeray and Dickens have to strangle their own feelings about sex with the unfortunate result that most of their heroines seem to have no character at all, and those with character like Becky Sharpe and Ethel Dombey have to be painted as a kind of villainess. Even writers as broad-minded and kind as George

Eliot and Mrs Gaskell have to punish their heroines who have lapsed from grace with the conventional fate of death or Australia or both.

Just how bold the Brontës were can be seen in the case of *Wildfell Hall*. Here Helen Huntingdon, the heroine, behaves with exemplary rectitude in, like Jane Eyre, fleeing from the temptation of adultery, even though her husband is a brute. It therefore seems unfair that Anne's novel should be accused of disgraceful coarseness. The coarseness in the eyes of the reviewers presumably took two forms. There is the frank admission that Huntingdon committed adultery with Lady Lowborough and Miss Myers, and there is an equal admission that Helen finds first Arthur Huntingdon, then Gilbert Markham sexually attractive. We have in the attacks on *Wildfell Hall* a clear statement of the extreme Victorian attitude that women should have no sexual feelings, and that sexual matters should not be mentioned.

Jane Eyre and *Wuthering Heights* may also seem to flout this convention, and indeed to do worse, since the conduct of Mr Rochester on the one hand, and Heathcliff and Catherine on the other, is not painted as particularly reprehensible. It is true that Jane Eyre herself displays considerable virtue in running away from Thornfield, but she had previously given offence by the uninhibited way in which she listens to confidences about Rochester's mistresses and dashes into his bedroom to rescue him from fire. Even before the first Mrs Rochester is revealed, Jane acknowledges that there is something not quite right about her early love for Rochester, saying that she was in danger of putting her love for the created higher than her love for the creator. Bertha Mason's lack of chastity and Georgina Reed's dissolute flirtatiousness are condemned. Jane still harbours thoughts of Rochester even when she has fled to Moor End, but one has to be very hard-hearted to condemn her for this. St John Rivers *is* so hard-hearted; one cannot help feeling that he is jealous and therefore hypocritical. The artistically cumbersome device of Mr Rochester's voice summoning Jane away from St John's proposal is a necessary way of rescuing Jane from accusations of improper behaviour in going back to Thornfield from which she had escaped to avoid a fate worse than death. Conveniently the fire at Thornfield provides a happy ending, economically furnishing Mr Rochester with a suitable form of punishment for his misdemeanours.

In all these ways, and in the way she ends the novel, not with the happily married Rochesters but with the martyrdom of the unmarried St John Rivers, Charlotte would seem to be leaning over backwards to accommodate Victorian morality. This was of course the morality she had learnt at home and school; her experiences with Monsieur Heger and her romantic Angrian fantasies may have shaken this, but they had not destroyed it. Modern readers have a very different morality and it therefore seems surprising that the reputations of both *Jane Eyre* and *Wuthering Heights* are still as high today as ever.

These reputations have suffered odd fluctuations. *Wuthering Heights* was not really appreciated until the end of the nineteenth century, when Mrs Humphry Ward in her prefaces to the Haworth edition, clearly placed Emily in a higher category than Charlotte as a novelist. Oddly Mrs Ward, herself a bestseller in her day whose sales far exceeded those of Charlotte and whose most famous novel, *Robert Elsmere*, aroused more controversy than *Jane Eyre*, is now almost totally forgotten even in academic circles. *Jane Eyre* in the first half of the twentieth century still had a popular appeal, especially among children, but among academic critics tended to be dismissed as melodramatic, romantic and incoherent. Meanwhile Emily Brontë's reputation rose. In the last forty years we have moved away from the shadow of the Victorians and are able to view them objectively. Charlotte, the more obviously Victorian of the two sisters, has gained from this new distancing. There is a danger, however, that we ignore how very un-Victorian the Brontës were in their social and sexual views. This chapter has tried to show how the novels were published and how remarkable it was that they reached publication at all.

10

Shirley and *Villette*

The details of the disastrous year 1848–9 in the lives of the Brontës are so well known as to need only brief rehearsal. First Branwell fell ill, and died in September 1848, a wreck of his former self. Emily took cold at his funeral, but she also seems already to have been in the grip of some kind of psychological malady which warped her and eroded her will to live. *Wuthering Heights* may even have forecast such an end. Within a few short months Emily sank into total apathy as her lethal cough became worse. She refused to leave the house and would not accept medical help. Charlotte tried every measure to aid her, even sending to London for a cure from a homeopathic doctor, but Emily would have no help from any such quarter. Her march towards death has been described as 'eager', but there seems nothing spirited about it. We might rather say that for some reason Emily sulked herself to death in circumstances which remain an insoluble mystery. The only explanation offered by those near to her was that she pined for Branwell: this seems a most unlikely hypothesis, and becomes more unlikely with careful examination.

A further mystery, linked to this, is whether Emily was writing another novel and, if so, what it might have been like. There is some evidence that she may have been and, just possibly, the plot was proving so intractable that she felt she could not cope with it. At any event, despite an attempt to write poetry early in the year, no progress seems to have been made with the novel, and this may well have added to Emily's despondency. It seems possible also that the conformity to death was one more aspect of Emily's desire to conform to the workings of Nature: in this respect she was a true heir to the Romantic tradition, and to the older one of the Stoics. A number of legends surrounding her death may be true or not; certainly she was so weak that she had difficulty combing her hair at the last, but seemed to cherish it still. Martha, the servant, told how she had dropped her comb into the fire on her last day and was incapable of picking it out of the embers. She died a little after midday on 19 December 1848, leaving Charlotte sad and curiously guilty: a guilt which was to be expiated in an odd way.

Meanwhile Anne was also ill. This was much more expected, since Anne had always been the delicate one of the family. Like Branwell and Emily she had tuberculosis. Unlike Emily, she was determined to fight the disease and arranged herself a holiday in Scarborough for the May of 1849. She lived just long enough to see her beloved seashore again, but died calmly on 29 May. Charlotte, as she later said, 'let Anne go to God'; she had never been particularly close to her and had always tried to treat her as a small child even when she grew up. One result of this mothering attitude of Charlotte's has been a disinclination on the part of the literary world to take Anne's work seriously; this disposition still remains. Charlotte was downcast at having to bury her sister at Scarborough, the only one of the six Brontë children to be exiled in death. She had tried hard to persuade Anne not to reprint *Wildfell Hall* and remained opposed to reissuing it now that she was the sole survivor of the family. The other relics, both of Emily and Anne, she seems to have cherished, and would shortly be seeking ways to add to their immortality.

Before the shadow of her brother's and sisters' illness darkened Charlotte's life in 1848, she had been mapping out a new novel. She knew quite well that it must be different from *Jane Eyre*, that it could not compete. It was to be set in the past, as all Brontë novels had so far been, but unlike them it would begin to come to terms with the industrialisation process, at least as a side issue. There is unfortunately very little on record of how the Brontë sisters felt about contemporary industrialisation or the social changes associated with it. *Jane Eyre* could be read as indicating that they wished to disregard it and turn instead to the related theme of how mankind could live in harmony with Nature. But the novels of the 1840s had put the historical process firmly on the agenda. Charlotte seems to have felt that she could not ignore it. She recalled stories told by her father about the days when he had first been a curate in the West Riding, at Dewsbury and then as incumbent at Hartshead. These days, just before the birth of the children, had been turbulent and were noted for the revolutionary activites of the Luddites. As she thought back, Charlotte apparently felt that her father's memories, and her own topographical knowledge, could be used to produce a telling new novel.

In order to be sure of the detail of the Luddite riots in the West Riding, Charlotte sent to Leeds for the file of the *Leeds Mercury*.[1] She told Mrs Gaskell that she had not discussed the plot or the characters with anyone. As the work was begun early in 1848, well before the deaths of Emily and Anne, this may reveal something about the decline of the traditional cooperation between the sisters at that time, but possibly Charlotte had forgotten any conversations she may have had with her sisters. The writing of the novel was sharply interrupted by Branwell's death in September 1848. For the next nine months Charlotte could only tinker with it during moments when it seemed that one or both of her sisters might survive.

Not until Anne had lost the battle for life at the end of May 1849 did Charlotte resume in earnest. Mrs Gaskell says that the first part written that summer was 'The Valley of the Shadow of Death', the first chapter in Volume III. By this time, the characters of her dead sisters were creeping into the personalities of Shirley and Caroline, a process to which Charlotte eventually succumbed and admitted. Shirley was, she said, 'what Emily Brontë would have been, had she been placed in health and prosperity'.[2] In some ways this grafting on of Emily's characteristics to the character of a girl already taking shape on paper enlivened the character, giving her some unusual traits which persuade us of her reality. But in other ways, the attempt was bound to lead to difficulty. Emily Brontë was not an heiress and it is hard to imagine her as one. Charlotte's amalgam does not always prove convincing.

Meanwhile, Caroline began to acquire characteristics of Anne, though she was perhaps in part based on Ellen Nussey and in part on an Angrian heroine, Elizabeth Hastings. Her eye colour changed and her behaviour began to conform to Charlotte's view of what Anne had been. In February 1849, Charlotte sent the manuscript to her publisher, a sure sign of her nervousness in presenting it. It was returned with encouraging comments, but could not at that time be regularly continued, such was the pressure of Anne's illness on her sister. It is doubtful, however, if it would have flowed like *Jane Eyre*; though there was a great deal in Charlotte's mind that would form the basis of a novel, she still had to come to terms with much of her material. Her final manuscript shows signs of hesitancy and slips of memory; but perhaps we ought to be amazed that the book was produced at all.

Shirley was published on 26 October 1849 and Charlotte braced herself for the opinions of the press. It was largely favourable, sometimes enthusiastic. Comparisons with *Jane Eyre* could not be avoided. Some critics were struck by *Shirley*'s dissimilarity to the earlier novel. *The Atlas* said 'it is not another *Jane Eyre*'; the irresistible spell of Charlotte's earlier work was missing this time, though there were resemblances. 'There is a wild north country landscape ... and a somewhat rude state of society obtaining in the neighbourhood.' On the whole, the magazine thought that *Shirley* was better written, there was less power in it, but neverthe-less 'It has the stamp of genius on it'. The *Examiner* disagreed, saying that the peculiar power of *Jane Eyre* was 'repeated ... with too close and vivid a resemblance'. The writer praised the new book for its vividness, directness and power of graphic delineation.[3]

A very encouraging review, printed in the *Standard of Freedom*, was written by William Howitt. Charlotte was surprised to find such encouragement 'from a dissenter' as she wrote to her publisher, W. S. Williams. Clearly, she considered she had attacked the Non-conformists too harshly to be forgiven. Howitt saw the similarity between *Shirley* and *Mary Barton*, though he noted that Mrs Gaskell was more likely to be at home among the working men and Currer Bell among the masters. This observation does reflect something about Charlotte's approach to life, a vein of social consciousness which we have traced to her father's efforts to better himself, and his feeling of social difference in his marriage to Maria Branwell.

An early result of the review was a letter from Mrs Gaskell herself. 'The note brought tears to my eyes', Charlotte reported. This was the beginning of a friendship which would issue in Mrs Gaskell's biography. Charlotte also asked for a copy of *Shirley* to be sent to Harriet Martineau, and this was done. A cheering letter was received in thanks and thus a further contact with the literary world was established. Though Harriet Martineau was to profess reservations about *Villette*, there was a great deal in common between the two authors. A further correspondent was G. H. Lewes, to whom she wrote back regretting that he had detected that she was a woman. The Bell nom de plume was far from being abandoned and at this time Charlotte clearly felt that it was better to remain ambiguous; many readers and reviewers had thought she was a man and so she wished it to continue.

Nevertheless, this group of encouraging letters persuaded her to consider returning to London, a place of mixed fortunes. Charlotte never really seems to have felt like a Londoner; she continued to see herself as a provincial on a visit. Emily, it must be remembered, had declined to go to London to deal with her publisher at all, and Anne had travelled there mainly as Charlotte's companion. Charlotte's comments do indicate a little curiosity to see the London literary world, but less taste for it when she arrived. She went up by train on 29 November 1849, primarily to visit the Smiths, by whom she and Anne had been kindly entertained during the previous year.

Throughout the visit she remained acutely nervous at meeting literary personalities. At times she was so agitated that physical symptoms of sickness assailed her, similar to those suffered by Emily as a girl at Roe Head: she went white, suffered headaches and nausea. The same malady had been with her in Belgium; she was later to describe it to advantage in *Villette*. As a result of this hypersensitivity, her first meeting with Thackeray was frigid and sterile. We have two versions of the encounter, one from the publisher George Smith and one from Charlotte herself in a letter to Mr Brontë.[4] The former notes that Thackeray quickly made allusion to *Jane Eyre*, exactly what Charlotte feared; she had told her publisher she wanted no allusions to her novel. It is hard to see what she might have expected, since her whole reputation rested on the book, and of course other people, including Thackeray, would want to discuss it with her. To her father she described Thackeray as 'a formidable-looking personage' whose conversation was sometimes 'cynical, harsh and contradictory'. It seems surprising that Charlotte could not detect that this was Thackeray's cover, just as sickness and headache was her own. In a sense, the apparent naivety of her reaction was the strength of her books, which appeared so direct and strong to the public. On paper, her intense shyness melted, but it would have been impossible for her to give herself away so freely in real life.

Meanwhile another public was found in the industrial villages of West Yorkshire. The area round Dewsbury and Hartshead had been familiar to Charlotte all her life, partly through her father's narration, partly through her own school life and later teaching engagement at Miss Wooler's school. Here she had formed friendships with a number of contemporaries: Ellen Nussey and Mary Taylor of course, but also the Walkers and Ringroses, Dixons and others, who came from the industrial families Charlotte had portrayed in *Shirley*. Some of these families began to recognise their own members in *Shirley* and in general approved. From this point on the Brontë novels became especially susceptible to the hunt for non-fictional origins, a game which can be taken too far. Shirley, for example, plainly was not a precise portrait of Emily, any more than Helen in *Jane Eyre* had been an accurate snapshot of Maria, though at times Charlotte seemed to give credence to these identifications. The Taylor family, for instance, recognised themselves as the Yorkes. In due course Charlotte's old friend Mary Taylor would write from New Zealand to comment on the good general likenesses, except that Charlotte had not made her father honest enough! In the period after the publication of *Shirley*, the whole Dewsbury–Birstall district seemed to be in a ferment of excitement.

But Charlotte's feeling that she must do something to ensure the memories of her two sisters did not ebb when she had transformed them in her new novel. She began to consider how best to present their work; the poems, *Wuthering Heights* and *Agnes Grey*, not, of course, *Wildfell Hall* which had so shocked her that she called it 'an entire mistake'. The poems had sold so badly that in 1848 they had been taken over by Smith, Elder, rebound and reissued as a 'second edition'. Sales now picked up and the reviewers went to work again. This alone did not satisfy Charlotte, who still felt there was a need to project the two sisters in a favourable light. In her loneliness she found it hard enough to envisage life without them, and she still saw her own literary enterprise as in part a joint one, in which Anne and especially Emily must still play their parts.

Accordingly she began to look over the bundles of manuscripts left by Anne and Emily, intending to select some more poems to add to a new edition that had been proposed. It is sometimes suggested that she weeded out the manuscripts, destroying Gondal material that had survived the sisters' deaths. This seems unlikely; the early magazines and other juvenilia of herself and Branwell she did not destroy, so why should she have done so in the case of her sisters? It seems much more likely that Emily and Anne had come to a sad decision during 1848 that their childhood inventions had now outlived their usefulness. Anne had for some time felt that they did not sufficiently face the real world. Some time during that gloomy autumn of 1848 she may have persuaded Emily to share her view and burn or bury the lot, except for the poems each had copied out into small notebooks, and a few scraps of earlier drafts and copies which may have survived because they were kept with the copy-books.

Of course this is speculation, but it is certainly true that Charlotte chose the additional poems for the edition she planned from copy-books, not manuscript drafts. One poem of Emily's only, 'Often rebuked', appears to have been copied from another source. As the year after Anne's death wore on, and Charlotte had been emptied of her new novel, she increasingly bent her attention towards these poems and a new version of *Wuthering Heights* which would avoid the 'blemishes' the early edition had exhibited.

The truth is that Charlotte was puzzled and even a little embarrassed by *Wuthering Heights*. As we have seen, she aimed for fidelity in portraiture herself, and rejoiced when she felt that both in *Jane Eyre* and *Shirley* she had been true to life. But Emily's inner life was a different matter. Charlotte had always recoiled from it and had consequently been shut out by her sister. Though she had accepted the general view that Emily was the genius of the family, her genius had sometimes been uncomfortable, sometimes bizarre, and Charlotte did not quite know what to make of it. She had once emitted the extraordinary opinion that 'Ellis will not be seen . . . . until he is seen as an essayist'. She now began to plan improvements to the novel, and three expiatory notes and prefaces to the work to be reissued.

It is interesting that Charlotte felt no scruple in modifying Emily's work and the poems of Anne which she now proposed to add to those printed in 1846. Manuscript additions to Emily's 'B' copy-book, the Gondal book, show that she did not immediately decide what to print, but added suggested alterations to a number of poems which in the end she did not choose. We have no manuscript of *Wuthering Heights* in any version, so that we have to judge Charlotte's editorial style from the 1850 printed 'second edition'. In the preface, she admits the 'rusticity' of the book; this caused her to modify the dialect phrases and to tone down some scenes considerably. She also comments on Emily's lack of knowledge of the actual people living around her:

What her mind had gathered of the real concerning them, was too exclusively confined to those tragic and terrible traits of which, in listening to the secret annals of every rude vicinage, the memory is sometimes compelled to receive the impress.

Thus one of Charlotte's aims was to normalise these characters in a small way. Her comments have some value as evidence, but we should beware of taking them at face value. During several of the most influential periods of Emily's life Charlotte had not been at home: when Emily had been exploring the moors in adolescence and becoming acquainted with the story of Ponden for example, and when Emily had kept house for her father in 1843.

Charlotte's editing of the sisters' poems proved to be erratic. In the case of Anne, she included a slightly altered version of a poem which had already appeared in the 1846 edition, *and* reprinted the same poem, so that two versions of the same work appeared in the same collection under two different titles. Whether this was due to haste or lack of care is uncertain. But in the end, the new selection of poems, some modified extensively, was offered to the public. Among the new works were Anne's 'Last Lines', very much altered so as to avoid the painful conflicts the poem had originally presented, in keeping with Charlotte's tender-hearted view of Anne; and another few verses from Emily's 'The Prisoner', rounded off by some lines of Charlotte's own. The poem does indeed present difficulties, and we understand Charlotte's feeling of the need for some mediation; but on the whole she caused more troubles of interpretation than she solved, especially to later generations who are looking for what Emily really meant rather than what Charlotte would have liked her to mean. This process, Charlotte told Ellen, was to be regarded 'in the light of a *sacred duty*'.[5] The revision was complete by 2 October 1850, when Charlotte wrote to her publisher, W. S. Williams, to thank him for his support. The modified versions remained largely unchallenged until the painstaking work of C. W. Hatfield provided a new edition in 1941.

On 10 December 1850, the second edition of *Wuthering Heights*, with *Agnes Grey*, was published and when it was off her hands Charlotte felt able to take up an invitation from Harriet Martineau to stay at Ambleside in the Lake District. Here she met the family of the renowned Dr Arnold, who had transformed the public school system, including Matthew Arnold, who was to leave such a great impression on the British educational system, and add to the store of great poetry. He recalled that she was 'past thirty and plain, but with expressive grey eyes'. (Many people noted Charlotte's eyes; her Irish uncle recorded that they 'looked through you'.) In turn, Charlotte recorded that Matthew Arnold seemed foppish but that, on closer acquaintance, he improved: 'a real modesty appeared under his assumed conceit'. During the same visit Charlotte met the powerful and determined figure of Sir James Kay-Shuttleworth, who took her out for a number of drives in his carriage. Later, he visited her at Haworth, illustrating by his interest a certain vulnerable attractiveness that Charlotte possessed; this was not shared by Emily.

Undoubtedly Charlotte felt flattered by the attention she was receiving from men of affairs. She had always been acutely aware of the poverty of the family; only her father's stipend had stood between them and destitution. In earlier days, it had seemed that they must obtain sufficient practice and knowledge to become governesses; the first sign of retreat from this course is seen with Aunt Branwell's legacy, small as it was. With the success of *Jane Eyre*, Charlotte began to realise at last the possibility of maintaining a small regular income which might keep her and her father from complete ruin. In 1850, she began cautiously to spend money on improvements to the parsonage. Some of its modern features date from this time; for example, the present size of the small slip-room over the hall dates from Charlotte's alterations; she narrowed the hall to increase the size of the parlour, with consequent implications for the upper storey. In a small degree, her fame as a writer began to bring home comforts to Haworth, which had been sadly lacking in earlier days.

Charlotte had now 'arrived' as a writer. The old pseudonym of Currer Bell was completely discarded and she began to feel herself part of the literary scene, though she still felt reluctant to go into the London literary coteries. A developing friendship with Mrs Gaskell would eventually lead to the 'authorised' biography after Charlotte's death, and to the presentation of Charlotte as a provincial 'home-spun' genius. There was much in common between the two authors. As *Villette* began to take shape, Charlotte felt aware that she should not allow it to compete with Mrs Gaskell's emerging novel, *Ruth*. The publication of *Villette* was eventually held back so that *Ruth* could have the benefit of current reviews before her competitor emerged.

In planning *Villette* Charlotte seems to have been aware, too, of the difficulty of avoiding competition with her own best-seller. Once again she was to use a single girl as the heroine from whose point of view we should see the life of a governess. Would the story be simply a repeat of *Jane Eyre*? Charlotte was determined from the first to invent a different type of character, though inevitably the new girl, too, would partake strongly of Charlotte's own personality.

I can hardly describe what subtlety of thought made me decide on giving her a cold name; but at first I called her Lucy Snowe (spelt with an 'e', which Snowe I subsequently changed to 'Frost'. Subsequently I rather regretted the change, and wished it 'Snowe' again. If not too late I should like the alteration made now throughout the MS. A *cold* name she must have . . . . for she has about her an external coldness.[6]

In the new novel, the Belgian scenery was to be borrowed from *The Professor* which had not succeeded in obtaining publication. Charlotte felt she must write out these scenes again. This time, unlike *Jane Eyre*, there was to be no ultimately happy ending. Paul Emanuel may have been intended to marry Lucy, but if so the reader must work the solution out for himself. Charlotte deliberately leaves the ending vague. The wintry nature of this conclusion, with the wintry nature of Lucy, surely stems from Charlotte's own wintry experiences during the last eight years. Though her letters are full of pleasant chat, beneath the surface her spirit was congealing and her optimism ebbing. Throughout her letters to her publishers, we encounter examples of self-distrust and doubt as to whether she could ever reproduce the success of *Jane Eyre*.

The precise nature of Charlotte's attachment to M. Heger will never be clearly known, but certainly such warmth was never to be felt again. The desolation following on the death of Branwell, Emily and Anne, which Charlotte had learnt to absorb, was slightly lightened by the persistent recovery from minor illnesses of Mr Brontë himself. Nevertheless, Charlotte was often lonely and wished she had someone to discuss matters with, whether they were literary or otherwise. Unlike the other members of her family, she had apparently turned down several clear opportunities to be married. She had received proposals from Ellen Nussey's brother, from an infatuated curate and, since the miraculous success of *Jane Eyre*, from one, if not two, members of the publishing firm. James Taylor, in particular, seems to have been enthusiastic as a suitor, but Charlotte had decided by 1851 that she would not marry him.[7] It has always been a mystery that her eventual choice, Arthur Bell Nicholls, had little of the charisma of M. Heger or James Taylor, and in some ways seems to have had little in common with Charlotte.

Once *Villette* had been published, on 28 January 1853, the summit of Charlotte's writing career was left behind. The book itself was enthusiastically received; George Eliot wrote:

> I am only just returned to a sense of the real world about me, for I have been reading *Villette*, a still more wonderful book than *Jane Eyre*. There is something almost preternatural in its power.

Many reviewers echoed that sentiment. Only Harriet Martineau seemed to contradict the acclaim, giving her opinion that the book concentrated too much on love as an overriding factor in women's lives.

Among other reviews, the *Examiner* praised the sharp characterisation, a result of Charlotte's all-seeing eye. The reviewer was critical only of the main character, Lucy herself, whom, we have seen, Charlotte intended to be as cold as she appeared. He traced this to personal experience on the part of the author and, of course, it did reflect both Charlotte's excitement and her despair in Belgium. The *Literary Gazette* pointed to Charlotte's 'charm of freshness' which is infinitely delightful. The thoughts of the book were the author's own. Like several other reviews, this one stressed the fact that the plot was not particularly unusual or new; but the intensity of feeling emerging in the book was almost universally approved.

Harriet Martineau was not totally misguided. In the Brontë novels, 'love' themes take precedence. Ever since the mid-1820s, perhaps before that, the Brontë children made love relationships between men and women their main concern. Even Branwell, who showed more interest in the details of exploration and in military questions, has many plots in his juvenilia and later writing (unpublished except in limited or scholarly editions, many years after his death) concerned with the theme of love. The chief source of this emphasis seems to be the Romantic poets whom they had read so minutely in early years. In real life, they found nothing to correspond with the heightened emotion of the poets and Romantic novelists. The sole survivor, Charlotte, had felt deep attachment to M. Heger, but this affection was bound to be futile. Since then, she had been attracted, apparently, to James Taylor, the publisher, but had refused close attachment. Now she was to change course and, in marrying Mr Nicholls, choose an unromantic, homely man with the qualities of steadfastness and determination, but nothing dashing about him.

Arthur Bell Nicholls had come from Ireland to be curate at Haworth during 1845, well before the deaths of the other three Brontës. A reticent man, he later gave almost nothing away about the family and only took to the public stage when he felt his wife's honour was at stake. For example, in 1857, after Mrs Gaskell's biography, he entered a furious controversy with descendants and supporters of Rev. W. Carus Wilson about Charlotte's accuracy in describing Cowan Bridge. Visitors to Ireland after Charlotte's death, when Nicholls remarried, spoke of his kindness and courtesy; but in some ways he seemed unsuited to Charlotte. Undoubtedly he had strength, but the enthusiasm and fire was concealed. It has always puzzled writers on the Brontës to account for Charlotte's acceptance of him when she did not take the more fervent James Taylor.

Nicholls' proposal seems to have come as a shock to Charlotte, not long after she had delivered what turned out to be her last completed novel to her publishers. Her letters to Ellen Nussey suggest that she had no intention whatever of accepting him at that stage and could hardly find any feeling for him in her heart. From the point of view of Charlotte's writing career, it is worth noting that her last two years or so are the least productive of any years since she had reached the age of ten. It is as though her passion ebbed away at the same time as her artistic genius, and she turned to Nicholls, the prosaic suitor, as she laid down her pen. There were to be two more attempts to begin novels (or two versions of the same novel), but scant progress was made with either.

At first Mr Brontë reacted wildly to the very idea of Nicholls' intentions. His apoplectic temper burst out and he frightened Charlotte into saying no more on the matter. It seems likely that the underlying cause was the feeling that Nicholls, an Irish curate, would bring the whole family back to the level from which

Patrick had worked his way up so many years ago on leaving for Cambridge. He had in fact misjudged the situation; Mr Nicholls' social status was a very great deal higher than the Bruntys of Ballynaskeagh. Nevertheless, he remained determined and it took over a year before his opposition could be overcome. It was April 1854 before Charlotte was engaged and 29 July 1854 before she was married. The marriage proved to be a death knell for Currer Bell in more than one way.

The question whether Mr Nicholls discouraged novel-writing has often been argued. In her biography of Charlotte, Winifred Gerin quotes a hitherto unpublished letter written by Mr Nicholls to Mrs Humphry Ward in which he records a conversation between himself and Charlotte after their marriage. In the letter he claims that he never interfered with her 'liberty of action' and maintains that they had discussed the fragment known as *Emma*, which Charlotte had begun in November 1853 and which made slow progress after that. Her husband had said 'the critics will accuse you of repetition', and Charlotte had said, 'O, I shall change all that'.

Nevertheless, the fragment did not progress and we may feel that, whether he intended so or not, Mr Nicholls was an inhibiting factor. Though clearly very proud of his wife, he was no man of literature and would have been unable to contribute to the kind of dialogue Charlotte had enjoyed with her sisters and brother; if she was happy with him – and he claimed that there had been no disagreements between them – it was a different, a more domestic and calmer happiness than that of artistic genius.

A further late fragment is known, consisting of the beginning of a story known as *Willie Ellin* from the main character. It is possible both fragments could have been attempts at the same story, or two parallel ways of working out the same idea in Charlotte's mind. Neither fragment was destined to become a developed novel and it seems likely that Charlotte did not write much during her months of marriage. She wrote several letters in which she spoke of her great happiness in marriage and the rumours that she had been unhappily married appear to have no foundation. Even after her marriage, she clung to her father as one flesh and blood relative who could provide a link with the cheerful days of childhood and family life. She was delighted when he and Mr Nicholls became reconciled and lived together in great harmony.

The pleasant comfort of the three of them was not to last. Less than six months after her marriage, Charlotte began to be ill with the self-same disease that had carried off her four sisters and her brother, tuberculosis. That she was probably also pregnant was no advantage in the struggle to live. No more than a few short notes to friends did the restless pen produce in those last four months. On 31 March 1855 Charlotte Nicholls died, leaving her father and husband to live out six more years together in the old parsonage. Nicholls kept her juvenile manuscripts and letters, with her sisters' poem manuscripts and various small records of the past. He thus became instrumental in preserving the Brontë corpus, and guarded it all jealously, as though he had been a literary man himself. Soon, he took the whole archive back to Ireland, bringing the wheel back full circle to the days before 1800 when Mr Brontë had been taking his first purposeful steps towards Yorkshire, and the creation of *Jane Eyre*, *Wuthering Heights* and *Wildfell Hall*.

Apart from the publication of *Villette* the most significant event of Charlotte's last few years turned out to be her incipient friendship with Mrs Gaskell. This lady soon cast a novelist's eye over Charlotte's home village, family and life history. Though she was wary of Mr Brontë, she had sufficient charm to be able to enlist his support in her project of writing Charlotte's life history; from some points of view it may appear that he was instrumental in fostering it. Yet he told Mrs Gaskell almost nothing and she was compelled to rely largely on the fond memories of Ellen Nussey, as were later Brontë biographers. Mrs Gaskell's sympathy with Charlotte, engaged during the last years of her life, was to grow apace when she began collecting material; in the biography she finished we are to some extent seeing a product of the combination of Ellen Nussey's faithful championship of her friend and Mrs Gaskell's novelistic skills.

This opaque lens through which we see the Brontës does some disservice to Charlotte, but more to Emily and Anne, if we are concerned to uncover a totally balanced version of their life histories. On the other hand, Mrs Gaskell's *Life of Charlotte Brontë* was a dramatic masterpiece, establishing for ever the Brontë legend. Nor is this legend to be cavilled at. Through it, the Brontës became living presences in their own works; the hunt for originals of their fictional characters and scenes began. In many cases, such originals were discoverable: Charlotte's all-seeing eyes had detected essential facets of the places and people around her, just as Mrs Gaskell herself was doing. Though this process can be taken much too far, it has enabled the Brontës' works to be mediated to a huge public ever since their deaths.

But Mrs Gaskell's short acquaintance with Charlotte, and the impossibility of recovering much about the lives of Emily or Anne, inevitably distorted the way in which the two other sisters might be judged; Charlotte herself saw to this with her partial understanding of her sisters combined with a fierce loyalty that would insist on putting them in the most favourable moral and artistic light. She had been their commercial manager in life, and the became manager of their posthumous reputations in death. Mrs Gaskell had no option but to follow Charlotte and Ellen Nussey. We in the twentieth century have been engaged in the lengthy task of removing the dusty glass through which the two other sisters are viewed and which, even now to some degree, colours public appreciation of *Wuthering Heights* and *Wildfell Hall*.

Notes

CHAPTER 1

1. E. C. Gaskell. *The Life of Charlotte Brontë* (London, 1855) and W. Gerin, *Charlotte Brontë: The Evolution of Genius* (Oxford, 1966) are still indispensable reading for students of the Brontës. Our two modern biographies (see below) attempt to correct their errors.
2. For Ellen's role in censoring the letters see T. Winnifrith, *The Brontës and their Background* (London, 1973) Chapter 2.
3. The two authors of this book are not quite agreed on the love affair between Anne Brontë and William Weightman, Dr Chitham thinking it probable and Dr Winnifrith merely possible.
4. The identity is taken for granted by some critics, but is by no means certain.
5. SHLL, Vol. II, p. 52.
6. Winnifrith, *The Brontës and their Background*, Chapter 7.

Suggestions for Further Reading

T. J. Winnifrith, *A New Life of Charlotte Brontë* (London, 1988).
E. Chitham, *A Life of Emily Brontë* (London, 1987).

CHAPTER 2

1. E. Harrison, *The Clue to the Brontës* (London, 1948).
2. The section on Mr Brontë's background is derived from E. Chitham, *The Brontës' Irish Background* (London, 1986).
3. The original P of the Irish version of the surname was softened in speech to B, and hence is spelt Brunty in some documents. It is thought that the change to Bronté and later Brontë was influenced by mimicry of Nelson's Italian title.
4. See *Jane Eyre*, Chapter 2; Emily Brontë's 'Aye, there it is!', 'How clear she shines!', 'To Imagination', in C. W. Hatfield (ed.) *The Poems of Emily Brontë* (Oxford, 1941) pp. 165, 184, 205.
5. Most of the information on Miss Branwell and her family comes from, E. Oram, 'Brief for Miss Branwell', *BST*, vol. 14, part 74, pp. 28 *ff.*
6. Details of Thornton are gathered in part on site, and in part from W. Scruton, *Thornton and the Brontës* (Bradford, 1895).
7. *Jane Eyre*, Chapter 12.

8. There are several accounts of the bog-burst and Mr Brontë's reaction to it. See, e.g. J. Horsfall Turner, *Brontëana* (Bingley, 1898) pp. 201–19.

Suggestions for Further Reading

J. Lock and W. T. Dixon, *A Man of Sorrow* (London, 1965).
E. C. Gaskell, *The Life of Charlotte Brontë* (London, 1855) especially Chapters 1–3.

CHAPTER 3

1. *Agnes Grey*, Chapter 10.
2. T. J. Winnifrith, *The Brontës and their Background* (London, 1973) Chapter 3.
3. C. W. Hatfield (ed.) *The Poems of Emily Brontë* (Oxford, 1941) p. 243.
4. CB to EB, 2 September 1843, SHLL, Vol. I, pp. 303–4.
5. CB to EN, 1842, SHLL, Vol. I, pp. 266–7.
6. CB to WSW, 23 December 1847, SHLL, Vol. II, p. 166.

Suggestions for Further Reading

O. Chadwick, *The Victorian Church* (London, 1970).
E. Jay, *The Religion of the Heart* (Oxford, 1979).

CHAPTER 4

1. B. Wilks 'Schools and Schooling in the Life and Literature of the Brontë Family', *BST*, vol. 95, pp. 355 *ff.*
2. J. W. Adamson, *English Education, 1789–1902* (Cambridge, 1964) pp. 347–86.
3. W. Gerin, *Charlotte Brontë: The Evolution of Genius* (Oxford, 1966) Chapter 1.
4. Diary Paper, 30 July 1845. SHLL, Vol. II, pp. 49–51.
5. P. Arch, *Education in Rural England* (Dublin, 1978) Chapters 2 and 3.
6. CB to EN, 11 May 1831, SHLL, Vol. I, p. 89.
7. Gerin, *Charlotte Brontë*, p. 65.
8. E. Chitham and T. Winnifrith, *Brontë Facts and Brontë Problems* (London, 1983) Chapter 6.
9. Quoted by H. C. Barnard, *A Short History of English Education*, (London, 1847) p. 183.
10. M. J. Quinlan, *Victorian Prelude* (New York, 1941) pp. 243–8.
11. *Jane Eyre*, Chapter 1.
12. *Jane Eyre*, Chapter 38.
13. *Shirley*, Chapter 7.

Suggestions for Further Reading

J. W. Adamson, *English Education, 1789–1902* (Cambridge, 1964).
H. C. Barnard, *A Short History of English Education: From 1760 to 1944* (London, 1947).

CHAPTER 5

1. *Wuthering Heights*, Chapter 3 and *passim*.
2. SHCP, pp. 231–2.
3. Recorded in E. C. Gaskell, *The Life of Charlotte Brontë* (London, 1855) Chapter 3. The date must be early 1824.
4. *Villette*, Chapter 2; *Jane Eyre*, Chapter 4; *Wuthering Heights*, Chapter 3; *Agnes Grey*, Chapter 4.
5. E. Chitham and T. J. Winnifrith, *Brontë Facts and Brontë Problems* (London, 1983) Chapter 6.
6. CB to EN, 4 July 1834, SHLL, Vol. I, p. 122.
7. Chitham and Winnifrith, *Brontë Facts and Brontë Problems*, Chapter 7.
8. C. Whone, 'Where the Brontës borrowed books', in *BST*, vol. 11, part 60, pp. 344 *ff*.
9. The Brontë music collection is housed at the Brontë parsonage.

Suggestions for Further Reading

C. Alexander, *The Early Writings of Charlotte Brontë* (London, 1983).
W. Gerin, *Branwell Brontë* (London, 1961).

CHAPTER 6

1. CB to EN, 24 August 1838, SHLL, Vol. I, p. 161.
2. Information concerning Law Hill and High Sunderland has been collected at Calderdale Public Library, Halifax and on site.
3. H. Marsden, 'The Scenic Background of Wuthering Heights', in *BST*, vol. 13, part 67, pp. 111 *ff*. E. Chitham, *A Life of Emily Brontë* (London, 1987) Chapter 9.
4. Charlotte appears to have been at Roe Head from 1835 to 1838, and at Dewsbury Moor from 1838–9. The date for the removal of Miss Wooler's school is often given as 1837, but the evidence for this is conflicting.
5. CB to EB, 8 June 1839, SHLL, Vol. I, p. 178.
6. *Jane Eyre*, Chapters 17 and 18.
7. CB to EN, 3 March 1841, SHLL, Vol. I, p. 226.
8. J. Whiteley Turner, *A Springtime Saunter Round and About Brontëland* (Bingley, 1898) p. 210.

Suggestions for Further Reading

I. S. Ewbank, *Their Proper Sphere* (London, 1966) Chapter 1, and *passim*.
W. Gerin, *Charlotte Brontë: The Evolution of Genius* (Oxford, 1966) Chapters 7–9.

CHAPTER 7

1. CB to BB, 1 May, 1843, SHLL, Vol. I, p. 297.
2. CB to EB, 29 September, 1843, SHLL, Vol. I, pp. 242–3.

3.   W. Gerin, *Charlotte Brontë: The Evolution of Genius* (Oxford, 1966) pp. 181–215. This research is excellent, but Miss Gerin equates fact and fiction much too readily in this chapter.
4.   E. Duthie, *The Foreign Vision of Charlotte Brontë* (London, 1975).
5.   M. Robinson, *Emily Brontë, A Memoir* (London, 1883).
6.   G, p. 139.
7.   SHLL, Vol. I, p. 307.
8.   SHLL, Vol. II, p. 1.
9.   CB to CH, 18 November, 1845, SHLL, Vol. II, p. 70.
10.   SHCP, p. 24.

Suggestions for Further Reading

E. Duthie, *The Foreign Vision of Charlotte Brontë* (London, 1975).
W. Gerin, *Charlotte Brontë: The Evolution of Genius* (Oxford, 1966) Chapters 13 and 14.

CHAPTER 8

1.   E. Chitham, *The Poems of Anne Brontë* (London, 1979) Introduction and notes, *passim*.
2.   C. Brontë, 'Biographical Notice of Ellis and Acton Bell'.
3.   Emily's poem manuscripts are chiefly in the British Library, the Brontë parsonage, and in various American collections. A number are still in private hands.
4.   Details of the publication of the *Poems* are based on G. D. Hargreaves, in *BST*, vol. 15, part 79, pp. 291 *ff*.
5.   *Shirley*, e.g. Vol. III, Chapter 4.
6.   Reviews collected by M. Allott in *The Brontës, The Critical Heritage* (London, 1974).

Suggestions for Further Reading

W. Gerin, *Charlotte Brontë: The Evolution of Genius* (Oxford, 1966) Chapters 16, 17.
E. Chitham and T. Winnifrith, *Selected Brontë Poems* (London, 1984).

CHAPTER 9

1.   E. Chitham and T. Winnifrith, *Brontë Facts and Brontë Problems* (London, 1983) Chapter 8.
2.   G, p. 314.
3.   The Clarendon edition of *Wuthering Heights* (Oxford, 1976), edited by H. Marsden and I. S. Ewbank, gives the details.
4.   Chitham and Winnifrith, *Brontë Facts and Brontë Problems*, Chapter 10.
5.   T. Eagleton, *Myths of Power* (London, 1975) Chapter 6.
6.   G, p. 20.
7.   M. Allott (ed.) *The Brontës, The Critical Heritage* (London, 1974).

8. T. Winnifrith, *The Brontës and their Background* (London, 1973) Chapters 5 and 8.

Suggestions for Further Reading

M. Allott (ed.) *The Brontës, The Critical Heritage* (London, 1974).
K. Tillotson, *Novels of the Eighteen Forties* (Oxford, 1953).

CHAPTER 10

1. T. Akroyd, *A Day at Haworth, BST*, vol. 19, part 96, 49 *ff.*
2. G, Chapter 28.
3. Reviews quoted in M. Allott (ed.) *The Brontës, The Critical Heritage* (London, 1974).
4. In the *Cornhill* Magazine, 1900, and CB to PB, 4 December 1849, SHLL, Vol. III, p. 54. There is no doubt about Charlotte's sincere admiration for Thackeray, which she showed by dedicating the second edition of *Jane Eyre* to him.
5. CB to EN, September 1850, SHLL, Vol. III, p. 166.
6. CB to WSW, 6 November 1852, SHLL, Vol. IV, p. 18.
7. CB to EN, 30 January 1851, SHLL, Vol. III, p. 205.

Suggestions for Further Reading

E. C. Gaskell, *The Life of Charlotte Brontë* (London, 1855) Chapters 18 *ff.*
W. Gerin, *Charlotte Brontë: The Evolution of Genius* (Oxford, 1966) Chapters 21*ff.*

Bibliography

Books on the Brontës

Alexander, C., *The Early Writings of Charlotte Brontë* (London, 1983)

Allott, M. *The Brontës, the Critical Heritage* (London, 1974)

Brontë Society Transactions (1896 and following)

Chitham, E., *A New Life of Emily Brontë* (Oxford, 1987)

Chitham, E., *The Brontës' Irish Background* (London, 1986)

Chitham, E. (ed.) *The Poems of Anne Brontë* (London, 1979)

Chitham, E. and Winnifrith, T. J., *Brontë Facts and Brontë Problems* (London, 1983)

Chitham, E. and Winnifrith, T. J., *Selected Brontë Poems* (Oxford, 1984)

Duthie, E., *The Foreign Vision of Charlotte Brontë* (London, 1975)

Eagleton, T., *Myths of Power* (London, 1975)

Ewbank, I. S., *Their Proper Sphere* (London, 1966)

Gaskell, E. C., *The Life of Charlotte Brontë* (London, 1855)

Gerin, W., *Branwell Brontë* (London, 1961)

Gerin, W., *Charlotte Brontë: The Evolution of Genius* (Oxford, 1966)

Harrison, E., *The Clue to the Brontës* (London, 1948)

Hatfield, C. W., *The Complete Poems of Emily Brontë* (Columbia, 1941)

Lock, J. and Dixon, W. T., *A Man of Sorrow* (London, 1965)

Robinson, A. M. F., *Emily Brontë* (London, 1883)

Scruton, W., *Thornton and the Brontës* (Bradford, 1895)

Tillotson, K., *Novels of the Eighteen Forties* (Oxford, 1953)

Turner, J. H., *Brontëana* (Bingley, 1898)

Turner, J. W., *A Springtime Saunter Round and about Brontëland* (Bingley, 1912)

Winnifrith, T. J., *A New Life of Charlotte Brontë* (London, 1988)

Winnifrith, T. J., *The Brontës and their Background* (London, 1973, new edition, London, 1988)

Winnifrith, T. J. (ed.) *The Complete Poems of Charlotte Brontë* (Oxford, 1984)

Wise, T. J. and Symington, J. A. (eds) *The Brontës, Their Lives, Friendships and Correspondence* (Oxford, 1932)

Other books referred to in the text or notes

Adamson, J. W., *English Education, 1789–1902* (Cambridge, 1964)
Arch, P., *Education in Rural England* (Dublin, 1978)
Barnard, H. C., *A Short History of English Education* (London, 1947)
Chadwick, O., *The Victorian Church* (London, 1970)
Jay, E., *The Religion of the Heart* (Oxford, 1979)
Quinlan, M. J., *Victorian Prelude* (New York, 1941)

Index

Ackroyd, Tabitha, 17, 23, 89
adultery, 8, 30, 32, 89, 94, 117
Aesop, 54
Africa, 5, 43–5, 54, 60, 65
Agnes Grey, 8, 10, 31, 34, 57, 75, 82,
  97, 109, 114, 116, 124, 126,
  135–6
Angria, 3, 43–5, 65, 85, 89, 105, 118
Arabian Nights, 54
Arnold, Matthew, 46, 126–7
Arnold, Thomas, 31, 40, 50, 126
Athenaeum, 106
Atlas, 122
Austen, Jane, 48, 94, 116–17
Aylott and Jones, publishers, 9,
  101, 109

Ballynaskeagh, 14
Baptists, 29
Beale, Dorothea, 40
Belgium, 7, 24, 28, 33, 37–8, 46–7,
  49, 51, 62, 68–9, 74, 76, 78,
  83–95, 97, 108, 128
Bewick, Thomas, 21, 63, 65
Bible, 18, 25, 29, 42, 45, 53
Blackwood's Magazine, 43, 54–5, 61
Bolton Abbey, 65
Bradford, 20, 68, 77, 80
Branwell Elizabeth, 1, 4, 7, 17–19,
  30, 40, 42, 80, 83–4, 88–9, 99,
  127, 134
Broad Church, 31
Brontë, Anne, 2–6, 8–10, 14, 16–19,
  24, 26, 31–2, 34–7, 44–6, 49,
  55–6, 58, 64–6, 68, 73–4, 78–9,
  81, 88–91, 96–103, 105–10, 112,
  117, 120–1, 123–6, 128, 134; *see
  Agnes Grey, Wildfell Hall and
  Passages from the Life of An
  Individual*

Poems: 'A Reminiscence', 107; 'A
  Word to the Elect', 17;
  'Domestic Peace', 103;
  'Home', 105; 'Last Lines',
  126; 'Vanitas Vanitatum',
  100–1
Brontë, Branwell, 1–10, 16, 18, 24,
  30, 32, 36–7, 40, 42, 55–6, 60–4,
  66, 75, 78–9, 81, 84, 88–91, 96–
  7, 99, 100, 102–3, 107, 109, 119,
  128, 136
Brontë, Charlotte, *for published
  works see Jane Eyre, Shirley,
  Villette, The Professor and Emma*
  other stories: *Ashworth*, 6,
  Caroline Vernon, 81, *Willie
  Ellin*, 12, 131
Poems: 'Apostasy', 92; 'At first I
  did attention give', 92;
  'Frances', 92; 'Gilbert', 92,
  107; 'He saw my heart's
  woe, discerned my soul's
  anguish', 92; 'Reason', 92;
  'Regret', 92; 'The Letter', 92,
  106; 'Where'er you go,
  however far', 54
Brontë, Elizabeth (sister), 4, 17, 41
Brontë, Emily, *for published works
  see Wuthering Heights*
Poems: 'A little while, a little
  while', 70; 'Aye, there it is',
  134; 'Cold in the Earth', 103;
  'Hope', 104; 'How clear she
  shines', 96–7; 'O Day! He
  cannot die', 107; 'Often
  rebuked', 125; 'Shed no
  tears o'er that tomb', 25;
  'Stars', 103, 107; 'The Linnet
  in the Rocky Dells', 100, 103;
  'The Philosopher', 98, 103;